WE'RE WATCHING HER SHOW:

(For Bathroom Sails Of The Starched Collar)

BOOK PUBLICATIONS BY JOHN PATRICK ACEVEDO:

We're Watching Her Show (For Bathroom Sails of the Starched Collar): The Ethos of John Patrick Acevedo (Xlibris Press, 2018)

Godzilla and Human Radiation: Global Poems (2012 - 2017) (Mill City Press, 2017)

Moral Authority: The Poems (2012 - 2016) A Gnostic Outsider Sociology (Mill City Press eBook, 2017)

Zen and The Carolina Clay: The Collective Poetry of John Patrick Acevedo (2016)

Waterloo Awakenings: The Gospel Stories of the Poetry of John Patrick Acevedo (2015)

Ice A.D. Apex Delivery: More Outsider Stories of the Poetry of John Patrick Acevedo (2015)

Weighing-In Authority's Conversion Spin: More Outsider Stories of the Poetry of John Patrick Acevedo (2014)

Deer of the Crossing Last Ones: More Outsider Stories of the Poetry of John Patrick Acevedo (2013)

Bad Technology and Poor Weather: The Outsider Stories of the Poetry of John Patrick Acevedo (2012)

Bubblegum, Slime, and Electro Man (original comic book, 2011)

WE'RE WATCHING HER SHOW:
(For Bathroom Sails Of The Starched Collar)

THE ETHOS
of
JOHN PATRICK ACEVEDO

To order additional copies of this book, contact:
Xlibris
1-888-795-4274
www.Xlibris.com
Orders@Xlibris.com
786857

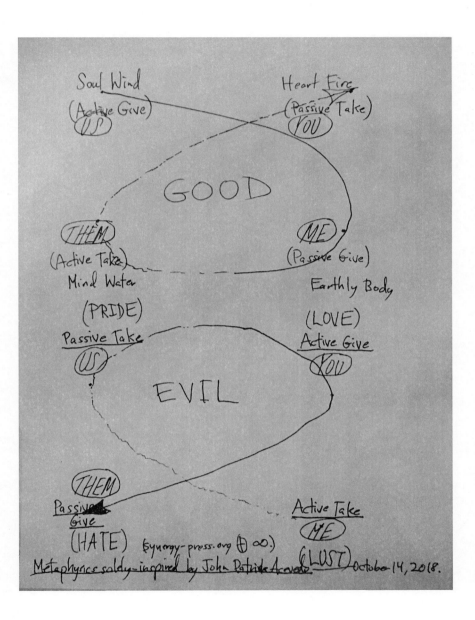

Soul Wind
(Active Give)
US

Heart Fire
(Passive Take)
YOU

GOOD

THEM
(Active Take)
Mind Water
(PRIDE)
Passive Take
US

ME
(Passive Give)
Earthly Body
(LOVE)
Active Give
YOU

EVIL

THEM
Passive Give
(HATE)

Active Take
ME
(LUST)

Synergy-press.org (⊕ ∞)

Metaphysics solely-inspired by John Patrick Acevedo. October 14, 2018.

To my best teachers, present family, loyal friends,
for fans of *"The Ascetic"*, the *Saints of Poetry,*
those who are Masters of "the hyperon"…
and to my late-father, Expert on the Physics of all worldly
things,
Mr. John Acevedo Maldonado.

"We're watching her show as the Police decease resistance of Baltimore girls that upgrade reality to outdated progress."

-John Patrick Acevedo, Poet., October 31st,'Halloween' 2018, Baltimore, Maryland.

"The Ascetic makes his mark as a born again arches poetry that grows dark with the have and hold of a life chosen like a mouth chooses to open for the poison of old presence left in the bottom of dust's glass with The Passion of splinter lust that bleeds like the mighty wound of God."

-John Patrick Acevedo, Poet.,

November 15th, 2018, 3:53 p.m.,

Columbia, Maryland

ix

Likeability Comments On Desperation's Heard

Everybody likes mercy. Nobody likes judgment.

"What a modern imbecile!" was all she said as I was blocked-off on both ends of a JetBlue flight.

My father finally insults with: "Do you have to do that right now?"

as he watches my sister's Daddy rub his 101% clothes the wrong way over custody battles.

I remember sitting in a room for rent until the chaos of order began.

Yet, never have I felt so unlikeable, in a non-violent sort of way.

I have never seen a job so prolonged, saw hyperons shave electrons from peace like a see-saw,

saw an odometer behind a son, a brisk walk to the last gate departing once more for Boston.

I look to my left, surprised to see a sack of jackets where two partners once had been,

the smile now gone, as progress forgets the entropy of perfection, like Eudora Welty's essay

"The Petrified Man", the comments of likeability spreading desperation like a party heard.

We never get it. We never have it... unless we don't want to give it back.

Vain you say? Perhaps.

But to live as humans we must lose purpose. Find your own struggle.

Seek out another's ever-elusive law and order. Make a mark on the sanctity of the child.

Baby, you know I'm kind of bad, so... my heart may get broken.

Yet the Word will get spoken. 'Cause someone will take your token' with their jokin'

and your Best Man will leave you cokin'. Believe in true memories. Buy the needs that End Game roads.

There's no exit to the path that always bleeds. If you wanna be free, forget the girl of your seed.

'Cause two and two together makes nothin' by marriage. You know, I'm a bye, bye baby, right?

Aimee Mann sang in "Red Vines" about watching her show while either at a drive-thru,

a drive-by shooting, or some drive-in movie claustrophobic car. Exactly which I cannot tell.

Smell as bad as you like. Learn something about acceptance, about prejudice.

I'm preaching in a booth at a Bob's Big Boy as a genius of bad trips screams: "Blasphemy!"

You know we push ourselves to be elited. Not that anybody's needed. If you beat the Four Seasons,

she'll dig with eye's deleted, like carpe diem digs fake Manning plays or Bono that girl with the journal in '85.

"Truth comes good enough for me because I've learned how praise is actively given and passively taken and prayer passively given and actively taken while art dies to the passive giving and taking of life's give and take activities. The worker is only an active to passive giver of lust. Market is always a passive to active taker of love. Pride and hate are our only salvation. For to save or to be saved, one need only to understand how the act of compromise breeds hope and those without fear are the children of a lawless fear."
— John Patrick Acevedo, Thanksgiving Day Blessing
November 22, 2018, 1:35 pm, Manteo, N.C.
synergy-pess.org ∞ John Patrick Acevedo, Poet.

Table of Contents

I. Unpaid Slash Church Visits:
"Let someone else get a chance."

II. **<u>No Sky Should Zone Ambivalence</u>:**
"Your father can't help you anymore."

POETS HOPE FOR FEARS PASSED

Foreword

by John Patrick Acevedo

On this Election Day, November 06th, 2018, ascetic, romantic John Patrick Acevedo is celebrating his acceptance of the offer by The New York Times to review his forthcoming poetry book entitled 'We're Watching Her Show: The Ethos of John Patrick Acevedo', (Synergy/Xlibris Press, 2018).

This is his Forward to be featured in it.

As Independent Sales Agent for Central Payment, a Californian ISO company specializing in merchant services, Poet John Patrick Acevedo recalls his three years at Boston University rather emotionally.

After many years with Best Buy, I saw a man wearing a grey Boston University jersey. I suppose one might think that this would help uplift my day, at the time I was #1 in both District as well as Store sales of high-margin attachments such as major credit cards, extended warranties, and such that earned me two Brad Anderson Legacy Stock Awards and countless MVA awards for Sales and Customer Service company excellence. Instead I felt an overwhelming sense of nostalgia. While at BU, I was more of a poet, albeit Professor Mandy Dyer at Clemson University deserves all the credit for helping me pride myself of my creative writing while a Freshman there the previous year.

However, during the late eighties, I was rather moved by things occurring such as the release of stellar films such like 'The Last Temptation of Christ', 'Star Trek V -The Final Frontier', and even Michael Moore's 'Roger & Me', not to mention the Dukakis-Bush final debate at The Ground Round Restaurant bar I frequented Friday and Saturday evenings before catching a latest release or deep conversations with a Sociology Theory Professor of mine who looked exactly like Anthony Perkins.

I began writing for myself in 1986, a morning I'll never forget, as it just happened to be the same one of my Freshman Class yearbook picture. I had a goatee at the time in homage of my hero Marvin Pentz Gaye, Jr., (I would actually sit in front of the same wall mirror that appears with him donning one in the two-time Grammy Awarded VH1 Pop #3 single "Sexual Healing" a day after my 27th birthday on February 21st, 2015 in the Casino Kursaal restaurant in Ostend, Belgium, where a bronze statue of him greets visitors during their artistic events on a weekly basis.

I lost a generous father, Physicist and scientist of world and higher things (MIT Physics Class of '67, "generous supporter of particle research on "the hyperon" with a B.S. Master's Degree from the College Park, MD School of Engineering at The University of Maryland as well as a 38-year engineer and computer programmer at Westinghouse, later Northrop Grumman), to an unexpected cardiac arrest on September 20th, 2014.

In the three and a half years that followed, I focused on Synergy Press instead, published the five next books of my poetry, did the business practices my father had always told me would "eventually pay off."

I suppose there are many things I could say about myself or even about my father, who, in my serious opinion as a practicing gnostic ascetic Christian is a Saint of Poetry. Yet all that matters now is having seen my Best Buy fellow employees pay beyond their means for a beautiful white ceramic Christian Cross flowered vase at my father's Puerto Rico funeral wake and viewing, giving a classic Synergy Press Waterloo Awakening Reading at Kozi Cafe in Rossmore Plaza, Silver Spring, MD, and seeing the love on the face of a business owner of antiquities after handing over my best Synergy Press books along with a Bonsai tree gift following the death of a close cousin from Jamaica Plain, Massachusetts and Sra. Ines Maldonado Acevedo, who had worked almost as long as my father for the island's U.S. Government, his very own mother.

Seeing BU finally recognize me in the Class Note I emailed Bostonia a few weeks ago is nice, yet what matters in life is not recognition. What matters is doing work that pays off.

John Patrick Acevedo was once a group organizer, attempted while a Junior and Senior to start a nonprofit organization he penned "The Organization For All People." He only received a single phone call the evening of his 'Big Open'. It was from someone who already had started a semi successful spiritual (Boston University is primarily Catholic although they preach a Congregationalist approach to Christianity) coalition.

Acevedo began his God, or rather "love", quest while a Freshman at Clemson University.

When "showing up" rather nervously to his VERY first college course, he was quite shocked to see a very beautiful Professor Amanda ("Mandy") Dyer.

Three years later, John Patrick, while alienating himself from "the human race", decided to be honest with at least himself and commit his life to poetry.

He had just completed a three and a half year straight reading (cover to cover) of the Holy Bible.

His late-father, Mr. John Acevedo Maldonado, believing his son was suicidal, offered help in the form of a major credit card, the convenience of his own car, the phone calls every day, and such.

Yet, Patrick was determined, now more than ever to 'get a job' BU at the College of Communication had guaranteed he would get.

As it went, he had just applied to an ideal (unbiased plush P.R. firm) job in Bethesda, Maryland.

He gave them his minimum expectation of $20,000.

"They would not offer me more than $17,000. I asked my father "Papa" what I should do. "Stick with it or to my gut or guns," I recall he told me.

Acevedo would never say never again.

Yet, in 2010, an African American slim-shady Supervisor would preach to him, as a jackal to a huge electronics retail chain to "promise [me] that you will at least give...[it] your best foot forward."

I had had to relearn how to walk again.

Instead, she motivated herself, wound up getting full Leave of Absence income when signing up with the Navy and lived in Guam as Acevedo had hoped to back in the Winter of 1990-1991 in a porch he rented in Forest Glen, Maryland from September 1990 until January 1991.

One evening near the end of his self-imposed exile, Acevedo had a revelation. He dreamt that the 'mystery of faith' all boiled down to one parable. It just happened to be the one that referred to salvation as a Herculean Effort. "For it is easier for a camel to enter through the eye of a needle than for a rich man to enter into the Kingdom of Heaven."

For him, this complemented perfectly his only other identifiable gnosis, which was "Vanity of vanities! All is vanity." (Ecclesiastes 1:2)

He believed that the Holy Bible was a book of secrets, like the Upanishads or the Secret Gospel According to Thomas The Apostle. Instead he got things about cubits, sacrifices, confusing blind faith.

At one point while a Sophomore at Boston University while renting a room in Orthodox Brookline, Massachusetts, he tried to commit to "writing poetry that was exactly the same as the Holy Bible." What happened next would, not only change his entire outlook on

Christianity, but on the purpose behind his vow of celibacy begun prior to being accepted at BU.

"I found that poetry needed to 'sound creative' not dogmatic."

Then, while a summer intern at the National Newspaper Association in Washington D.C., a Managing Editor and his sidekick Marine that kind of looked like Cher's ex Sunny Bono, introduced him to the unproven mineral aphrodisiac of his Marine days we know as 'saltpeter.'

It was that exact metaphor he had been starving himself for and that night on a toilet with a new responsibility to "watch the house" (his extended family were going to Rehoboth Beach without him for the first time) a poem entitled "Saltpeter is my Pillar."

"I had just the word 'saltpeter', you see. I prayed to God for the wisdom of a title for my very first poem. My memory as it turned out was weaker than Him." Acevedo placed his index finger randomly on a single word in his own Dictionary after shuffling its pages with his eyes closed. He opened his right eye and to his surprise his finger rested on the word "pillar."

Eudora Welty had been a favorite storyteller to Professor Dyer. She insisted on her class reading on their own her short story entitled 'The Petrified Man'.

But also the Book of Job. That was something Acevedo was learning to appreciate at the time.

"Want to go bobsledding?" This was the question his fellow student of Spanish 101 had asked him early in his second Semester at Clemson University.

It turned out to be 'Bible Study.'

Strangely, his family were products of the Hippie Movement when he was conceived in 1967.

His father was a loyal MIT student of Physics and gave his best to the university all of his life. Patrick was allowed to accompany him almost every other year to its Annual Weekend, something he was not supposed to understand was the reason his father would eventually never forgive his son for.

The Acevedo family was initially from Lares, Puerto Rico. His grandfather, a Trump-like Salesman inspired John Patrick Acevedo at a very early age. His own father had demanded that he clean up his alcoholism "just for Patrick," another family secret he never knew.

When John was 'feeling the Lent' effect of his first year of abstinence, Juan Acevedo Acevedo became either amused or impressed.

"I only wanted to be loved," he says. So "Papi", as his children called him, "cleaned up" over my foolish faith.

When Juan died, John Acevedo Maldonado was devastated. Not only would he have to face his own guilt of having betrayed his own father to go to MIT, but he would also have to betray his own family, included in the end, his own son.

A secret of the Acevedo family is that they "cannot die alone."

Juan wound up being physically released beside his father's girlfriend and daughter the night he finally went into Cardiac Arrest, the same way John, his son, had been on the night before a Leadership Conference at MIT the night he texted his concerned son Patrick "All is well." in a final text prior to his sharing news of his recent book's publication in a WhatsApp video that he marked as viewed the following morning with the same intent James Taylor suggests in his popular song called 'Fire and Rain', by sending it without knowing exactly "who to send it to."

"You killed him," was what his girlfriend accused him a few weeks after his death.

John Patrick Acevedo was blessed to know these secrets. Not told "to him but whispered around him." Acevedo was so sensitive, he could hear the birds begin gossip every morning, even while his nuclear family lived in several apartments in Berwyn Heights, Glendale, and later Laurel, MD.

Acevedo received a Boston hospital doctor's phone call in the late morning hours of September 20th, 2014.

Patrick started doing all of the things his late-father instructed him to do in spite of his disappointment with his inability to respect him best interests.

Acevedo is not "paranoid" or "thief" so far as his purpose in life goes as some claim. Like his father, he gave a company "best twenty years of his life."

"When I lost my Dad, I didn't want to die."

So, on the day after my twentieth anniversary, I was given the gift by my great General Manager, to come in "to discuss my options" to retire on the day following my twentieth anniversary.

"Moving on," was the exact entry into the company's HR portal that day.

Since 2014, Acevedo published five more books on his own Web Page, and even several video poems he then posted onto YouTube.com.

He had changed.

Yet he admits that he now accepts himself. His family, all but fragmented with his decisions, revealed the final secret when his grandmother finally partly endowed him with her son's inheritance.

"I felt betrayed," Acevedo says. "My closest relatives, old friends, even some of my neighbors, seemed amused by my flamboyant taking of risks and hid their amusement with my ascetic acts of survival."

He was alone.

After several unsuccessful years of taking "The Devil's License" exam for Life and Health Insurance (he passed the State portion almost immediately), Acevedo developed gradual hemoglobin complications, due to an extremely low dose of an isotropic medication he insisted on taking to help him sleep.

"I was nicknamed 'Tiberius' in the intensive care unit in September of 2017." His blood sugar well over 1000. He had survived three years and four months without any central heating in his new home. "I suppose it's poetic justice."

"You have to suffer to be an artist," Marvin Pentz Gay, Jr. (Motown's greatest artist Gaye) was reported in the papers as saying the day after he died of regrets. "You can't write about suffering and love unless you've don't it. And let me tell you.... I've done it!"

As to his own suffering, Gaye reportedly said in his final words: "Father hates me. I'm going to pack up my things and leave and I'm never coming back!"

It is sad how life always benefits the needs of the many over the needs of the few or the one.

And yet, this year, 'Free Solo', a National Geographic film that demonstrated Acevedo's own ambitions, ('Star Trek V - The Final Frontier' had Captain James Tiberius Kirk scaling 'El Capitan' during it's opening credits in 1989), demonstrated that, like his faith in Jesus Christ being "within not without" could accomplish anything in time.

I cannot impress upon you enough how much effort and empathy Acevedo has put towards 'We're Watching Her Show: The Ethos of John Patrick Acevedo.'

All we can conclude from his success is that he survived for some purpose void of broadcast echoes.

"I only wanted to please my father like my idol Marvin Gaye," he says. "The problem with life isn't that we are somehow Damned or Saved. The problem is that we reward neither the victim or the hero and confuse them to be without the truth about ourselves."

If Patrick could say that he was a Bastard to his family, he would probably be much happier than he was before he lost his father to his inability to ask him for help.

"If you ever are in need of help, just ASK me for it... or ask ANYONE. Do you understand?" his father tells his frightened son the morning he has him drop him off at the airport just before being betrayed by his own fear of mortality.

"I regret this whole thing terribly," Acevedo says.

I wish he was with me. I wish I could be with him. We were the same, he and I. That's the problem. My salvation is that now you know Him. A true grandson, son, father, and the ascetic's Saint of Poetry.

John Patrick Acevedo introduced Maryland to his theme of "give and take" (Book of Job, Old Testament) while a regular at poetry open mics, among them 'The Mariposa Center for Creative Expression' (February, 2003), where he was first featured with his book entitled 'Everlasting Chemistry.'

He remembers the event rather fondly, explaining his need to engage the audience by listening to an audio cassette in his car while driving so as to know his poem selections like the back of his hand, laughing as he recounts quickly praying to God for balance even as he stood up at the very end of his delivery as the podium his work rested upon was on a wooden floor sprucing a microphone cord and a crowded stool.

"My poetry had initially bookended many Facebook texts to a friend from 2010 to 2012. 'Bad Technology and Poor Weather: The Outsider Stories of the Poetry of John Patrick Acevedo' seemed to simply be a result of spiritual torture that I was going through on a daily basis to stay strong with my numbers. Still, I really got a rush from beating my own standards of excellence, only surpassed by the poetry I shared while there over energy drinks and meds that made me into a sort of Godzilla and King Kong hybrid, depending upon what you consider is a better metaphorical monster of high-margin sales.

Nevertheless, surviving these days were perhaps the proudest moments of my life. Unfortunately, for both me and my even greater late-father, poets hope for fears to pass by the stress of passing numbers, like faith passes doubt and black passes red, especially in the last hours of every month's last week."

There on the inside of their corporate walls of a Bush-American war over Terrorism, a tired virgin sits long hours alone, prints sign batch after sign batch, does the math he hopes will eventually pay off.

He knows his company's logo stool will one day sit in his own kitchen somehow although he never thought it could arrive after paying the highest price for it as cruel charity.

You can't change people. Accept yourself. Sadness comes from easy, not from hard.

Change instead your stubborn attitude. It may sound fast at first, yet your fate and the fate of the human race will depend upon your slow progress.

I have played its game and I have won.

I win for my heroes. I win for the ones who tried to make me believe in more than just a sign over the timeclock that reads: "I BELIEVE."

Another small door swings open like a good dream. I am told that I am now a part of the human race.

Yet there is one among them who knows me better.

I walk with her for a time as my own father still thinks he is doing the right thing with this constructive eviction, celibate opinion of my need for "Soul Attraction."

I think he was right to have that social worker slapped in the face by his parent's Old Man.

I think if I was told, after begging for possibilities that my "disease" has no cure, I would have done the same thing.

The Old Man is going home.

"A liability," the security officer had said as I prepared to see my father on what would turn out to be my Last Hoorah.

The one who knows me better than him had asked me twenty years before, after a surprised confession by me, if I can guess what is her real name. "Woe... man." she says.

I. <u>Unpaid Slash Church Visits:</u>

"Let someone else get a chance."

Really Naps the Maitre D
(for my grandfather Juan Acevedo)

At sea, we mask beneath the mirrored cascading,
the mask we don whenever we kiss and pass parading.
I see her tears like salt in the earth sweats a bed;
see her years outclassed by mine
a hair and a breath.
She climbs out of her mattress way,
way ahead. I am retired,
an uncrumbled wall of work fame.
At sea, really naps the Maitre D when pics keep asking
exactly just what grade of milk drowns
the silver pitcher, as he pours grease like a home plate
is run by El Nino's curving, checkered legged referee sliding catch.

I am listening to *'Red Red Wine'* by Neil Diamond
like it was *'The Summer of '89'*.

Somehow, he sings my sadness way too high,
leaves me laughing
like a serious, misunderstood clown.
Could I forget the slamming
morning door my Senior year by the Russian roommate?
Can I go back to the issues I've outgrown
like my unrepressed adolescence?
Stay with me an hour or two as *'September Morn'* plays
in my stateroom's backseat.
I wrote you this note to say 'Thanks' for the year
God barely forgave.
The ship sways as I point
my text steering wheel into your finger paint, ocean moon.

Whatever you say, Dear.
I'm beyond effort, beyond the balcony's ballad spreading friendly fire.

1

'Heartlight' has E.T. phoning home after a much-too-long delay.
He found a friend. Maybe I can, too.
My cell phone gets weaker like your biological clock
loses charge of my battery unconnected.
What I mean to say, the Maitre D already said
by the justice shining in his front car seat teeth: God's eye
immunity parachuting, dropping lines
like lies shake us to our fist's church immunity.
Holding onto to love's return is like letting go of a life lived too near.
It means nothing but the regret
of forgetting all but that which makes us plain.
Don't explain the tragedy of unabsorbed misperceptions.
I feel your mercury lust in the lines I drop, like whispering dust
collects impersonal space.

Broken Limbs
(for Michael Monk)

Avocado. Chocolate. Cheese. My doctor prescribes me something to drown this energy.
"Excuse me?" says the housekeeper as I complain about her unplugged lamp lightbulbs.
She waits as my red lobster face and thinning, broken-limbs salt drip something wicked.
The secret of success feels less like failure as I paper sweat cream over curling toenails.

If I'd thought life was going to go from love to lust to pride to hate, I'd have thumbed broke.

It doesn't show but the cops park outside the just-closed bank drive-thru for local reasons,
not for these tourist porn soles horn torn socks another day as John Lee Hooker explains:
"You left me once. You'll leave me again." I was hanging on for the hold-out sun of dream
when a door slams for pizza like a poem or limbs mousetrapped on cancelled plastic seats.

I was holding-out for the hanging-on rain when I heard that Berry Gordy was concerned
about sales when he asked Marvin Gaye to overdub Tammi Terrell on her first #1 duet.
Yet in 1967, America was dysfunctional love and life a messed up, down and out family.
I drive up a road in Hanover, Virginia, test the 1729 *Slash* latch on a first fellowship door.

If I'd thought life was going to go from love to lust to pride to hate, I'd have thumbed broke.

Bad Technology and Poor Weather

I'll be looking up meanings in my college dictionary
until I find out the mysteries the tallish borrow so that we can talk.
I'll be jogging footsteps by a machine my father once sought;
puffing fog Rocky Balboa and I lost when my thoughts were soft.

They say art is the path of greatest ease.
Eventually, even fools realize that this world is all we got.
I say bad technology and poor weather work together
like a pimp with lust and love without a main squeeze.

I am the forest of fallen trees, a river of rolling logs.
I am the unbelieving Christian, holding a stick at a church picnic:
circling like a cat in a corner as children chase unrequited dogs.

They say art is the path of greatest ease.
"Lover please don't forget my lot."
I say it's only poor weather that makes technology's cure its own
disease.

She was looking out of the limousine window;
impatiently waiting for her bridal door to chop.
Still, it was she who called up Daddy for the flowers
when my cousin's casket was briefly opened for his Pops.

They say art is all about absent presence.
I say it's in the present absence that moments seize
when danger's poor weather becomes beauty's bad technology.

If love were an accident, I'd be the first victim lost.
If love meant fighting, I'd be the soldier who moved the line only to
be shot.
Life is no fish story. It's always better told after the fish has been
caught.

Mornings are for secret wishes; evenings for news the world has forgot.
Only want to say "I love you." Don't care what my favorite critic thought.
Every spring begins with a rain that brings the lessons painful artists drop.

Whoever said art is the price that gains from the greatest debt was never a boss.
I say art is compromise, not to receive from the poor the wealth that suffering gets.
"Only imagined what they wanted." That's what a masterpiece used to cost.

Glasses and Nail Clippers (You're the Best)

I.

The Jimmy Kimmel thorazined credits sugar high with ten degrees, laps my pre-anniversary of three years and four months with non-relief.

My living room tray filled with hospital, toy-phone ordered Gov-grub, a familiar feeling takes hold, tells me the Intensive Care Unit just got a book.

I see the sinners sit holding hands on the corners of the pews,
waiting for their best friend to arrive.
I am near the pulpit dead center, both hands protecting my Bible.
I look up. The Catholic Church is brand new. It looks to me like a Hilton
I once checked into in Oxnard, California— a newly-painted, storage
monastery.
The Monks will soon arrive.

People started coming here in much smaller crowds after the diseases
of 1607.
Tobacco and coffee pitched across the Atlantic the irresistible
bargains in the trip.

She was beautiful when I Soap Opera honeymooned her. I remember
she cared most
when she forgot to balm her chapped lips. The night she invited me
to the break room,
opened the shared refrigerator, lifted tinfoil, showing her family
picnic's steamed crabs.
I remember the way she used to straighten her back as she snapped:
"Next customer!"

I remember the night she inhaled helium, tried to sound humorous
though she was not.
I can feel the recent cold that had almost fatally fragmented my thoughts.
I can hear and see the Weather Channel sing-song something about
the sun
coming or not coming out at the end of the week.

I had a pet collie as a child. He was much more loyal than most.
I since have come to understand that he loved me so much more
than I could bring myself to love him.

My Westinghouse, long-bearded father taught me in 1991 "give and
take."
Tried his entire life to cover for his ex and me every time we made
mistakes.
Every Christmas, showed me a smile as he watched me mystically
open gifts.

Maybe I have written too many poems of loss and paternal gain.
Yet this one sounds like me when I was again in an apartment with
ionic heat.

There is nothing precious when your family looks outside your
accustomed needs.
Only the past survives in the child's teacher pet chocolate apple
tombstone university.
The rusted side of the coin drops grades like the Spring's seeds,
like the earth flattens breathed ideas with society's business of fake
sugar and salt.

II.

Poco a poco God's "That's it!"
I once rented a room in Brookline, Massachusetts.

In one, a veteran from Vietnam lived with America's post-human radiation nightmares,
slammed his left palm on my grandmother's red Jello kitchen table.
Smiled as my head shot up for air like Joseph Conrad's: "The horror! The horror!"
Once I heard a scream. Followed the landlord spy up the winding oak stairs.
The next breakfast she said only one word that became his meds: "Bed-fire."
The City of Boston had fired him again. Us working Americans.

Try this. 4.0 grade point average from Composition 101 parts one and two.
Almost 50, my thumb must now take a prick. The Stop and Shop has been bought
by heels that bleed from dress shoes stigmata worn for the suitcase cab ride here.
My lived-up promise for Puerto Rican parent civility that still period's mattress sheets.
My periodic joke still beats the eggs as the landlord spy waits for the punchline,
as she dials my transistor radio to 'Rags to Riches', a gift from Metro's Andrew stop.
"Forgive me, Professor. With all due respect, what does that have to do with Mandy?"

I open the front door. "It's like a sauna in here…" Kramer should not have said this.
I feel the ground of my house, the still-gathering energies of third-party publication.
The thawing of my body heat motions and rests my blood feet.
Try this. Because just beyond finality's fear is hope.

Cat Stevens sang: "It's not time to make a change.
Just relax. Take it easy." Some, unlike me, have tried this.

Some pay with family. Others with traded life.
Some quit three jobs. Learn priorities.

I was scared of failure, like him.
Yet today I speak the language of glasses and nail clippers—
the lowest common denominator between father, son, God and man.
What we both chose to loose for survival's gain.

Because gain saves lives
knowing that loss, like life, has no breaks,
buys nothing but loss, sells nothing but gain.

The active give of indifference is a shame only the have's can
understand.
It is take's passivity that breeds foolish have-not's.

Glasses. Nail clippers. Struggle. Death.
Fate will try to change your fake.
Survive. There is no such thing as Holy sugar or salt.
Only the passive, active needled Cross that labors, sits, and thaws.

Return from fame's incognito loss and wake
with the fat that walks in standing water like old meat rot.
Prayer will inverse your praise thoughts.
So before Martha and Mary damn your BAM life;
before Judas lifts their well bucket,
kisses you on your insulin lips with lust's lucid frost,
try this. Because just beyond finality's fear is hope.

There is only one sugar for effort's REM-sleep.
There is only one salt for charity's unreal loss.

Despite the brimstone of my speak, my heart is full with life, love,
and work.
My mind woken from the broken down systems of my society.

Some say life is Glory Days. I say brush your teeth. Soap shower your hair.
If you try this, you just might say: "I was dying day by day."

The door stays open. I sit to return to the earth the thawing of personal bests.
I worked it out, poco a poco. Unlike the Hollywood Church saying: "Life goes on."

A squirrel rushes to a fictional sewage stomp.
The ants no longer gather at the corners of my doormat's woodshop project.
At my mailbox, the neighbor's dog speaks the language my father and I speak.
I have an old cat for a Pen Pal Zen. His other house a fire in which he bolts,
like the blackmail of its weather begins.

My collie had to learn my language of nine and a half half-life heat.
I loved him, yes. They say: "manic". He would have said: "Eso es un abuso."

It's the poison clouding every stew that brings the crowd with flowers to heal outside the fake sugar, Holy salt wounds.
Yet, the proud can only humble you if you become loud.
For the proud hate to live without being loved.
Only the meek can withstand their quiet, leave inhumanity in another's room,
as if they could justify being too tired of the most patient's 'now'.

My forehead is still covered by my moist toilet paper the morning of his anniversary.
The grace of God, I would say.
"Gov. Police," the bold shy nurse listens yet thinks this as I relay the Good News.

Hold onto your fear, dear extended family, despite not bringing hope
to Room 2206.
Sorry if I seem like my apparent father's Evil when I say: "Aced
Armageddon today."

Last night my sheets of damn endocrine earth were not thawing at
predawn first light.
He had waited for my procrastinated shift to arrive with his policy
of open-door Physics.
There are no breaks. The concept may be too hard for 'Hip Hop
Hooray Superbowl' plays.
The nurse took my ceramic bowl only because she wanted a break
from my shaved ice.
Which way leads to the Promised Land all depends upon the language
even animals speak,
like today's returning to sit on my doorstep without only the two
things
sit on the thawing of the salted pain of Old, the sweet pleasure of
New Testament wings.

Alas, unsweetened juice replaces ER's shaved ice.
So unlike the tea's Cat Stevens, so like Maui's Marvin Gaye.
"Try this. All he needs is two shots," says the man,
until the other side of the wall between us bangs from his fist,
as my dedicated medical team Darth Vader chokes him.
Never mind the budget. Never mind the insurance.

Guatama Buddha always knew what he knew.
No matter what they know they'll never know.
Because there are no breaks. Like there is no rise
or fall along the Christ bridge from charity to effort.

What we see through and what no longer remains
needs progress. What we forsake for grace and justice
needs the will that changes fate like fake sugar and salt.

My Church-going neighbors collectively open garage doors
at 7:45 a.m. as I smile, pocket a lost nail clipper from slanted ice,
press the frames of old prescription glasses against my eyebrows,
as poor weather freedom and bad technology sharing trucks garbage.

III.

My job position replacement did it to save me in 1995.
Vice-President Royce Reed did it to try to make me lose my celibacy.
The managers made me so mad, each time they paused at the door
to question my gnostic bush-shit attitude, I hated their New Age
freeloaded cd's,
the distributor handed from boxes inside a white van, told that they
were free.

Harder than Cream of Wheat. Harder than unrecycled liver's
saturating mud shit.
All night a body aching brother moans advice from the hall outside
his door to me.
C'est la vie. No makeshift plastic Iron Man arm shower armor for
his funnel IV.
A thousand sweet of blood after the Korean nuclear testing brought
Arctic Apocalypse.
Try this. My cell phone sends a blurry selfie from Room 2206 at one
percent.

I sit lopsided inside the wooden armrest of a couch, watch the nearby
roof's pipe
steam polluted gases from my plate glass window. Notice the feigned
non-security
behind grated blinds cranked half-open, recording the murderous
research philanthropy.

For the first time, the sky grows purple, and I am not listening as my wrist alarm rings.

The bell does not toll for me. My house bears the bitter cold like that of Dr. Zhivago's.

Returning sits on the thawing because sometimes the man needs you more than sympathy.'

The first night home, my pet collie shook on red Alice In Wonderland steroid pillows.

The polaroid picture of me sitting beside him in father bought pajamas speaks millions.

Yet, upon seeing it, my father decided to change the language of our domestic history.

I suddenly stand up from my front door's lip, do a 360 back inside the now lukewarm air.

I understand nothing about why they left me. But I am the quintessential pebble

stuck in your sock way down deep. I am the car keys of open-door Physics Office visits.

And he is speaking something new, something that even he can speak.

He is thinning invisible from our past's sacred mortality at last

as is the roof's pipe rusted exhaust of purple loss evaporates his dust into the sky.

Yet I have been crucified by three years and four months of healing's resurrected past.

He said to try this.

Saltpeter is my Pillar

Suffering in the hold of movement,
I remember the labor ahead of me.
My lips part and I swallow
as the future is passed again.
I never wanted this frailty;
never wanted the pain
that grips my brain like an alien.
But such is the healing of sanctity.
The cure is brine
stewed at a downtown meat plant.
It was either that or redemption
by the acid of grapefruit juice.
Understand. I do it
to be with Him.
For who else believes so deeply?
Who else can't even face
a woman's naked anatomy?
I've eaten away at my intelligence.
Turned it all to dependence.
The more you must let go,
the more you can follow.
That's the secret of my sacrament.
For just then I know the faith
that's lived, lacked, and lost;
know the transience
that always brings me back again
puckering with the taste of immortality.
Those covered by cult blankets
hour after hour,
learn to slow the motor's revving,
salt tomato heavens with promises
twenty-four seven,
tiptoe coal like Jesus walked water.

14

Animal Security

She was gone.
Only pain lingered,
a sign
of the pleasure that was taken from her.
"Be good," she had said;
her fingers raking my skin
like those of Master
while my nails would slide, scratching the tub.
He eats and sleeps in a corner now;
afraid that she might return.
Barking at Him,
I beg for the scraps upon His lap.
Yet all He does
is lift His eyelids:
ever-dreaming
of having a new mind to tame.

The Missing Rib

I'm blinded by a person I'm seeing now;
my emotions for her never quite spent.
I feed off all of them to set her free,
like the hunger that came and went.
My claim is the past she shares with me
and the future we've let will unfold.
For to possess His present is to only live
for weak times hopes and fears make bold.
She depends on me to heal my heart
that I may use it in her time of need
and teach myself what she has learned:
that to succeed in love, we have to lead.

Grief Grace

(for Gina)

So weak I could cry.
So proud I could lie.
Yet in you I find the courage to ask
for everything I've lost.
For doubt keeps me to the task
of picking up where you left off.
And grief teaches me grace
that trades loss for gain—
if I stick to what I'm missing
though I'm too weak to laugh,
though I'm too proud to speak the truth.
Yet it's in these moments
that you become my strength.
It's at these fleeting times
that I'm worthy of your honesty.
For it's been you all along
who tasks me into asking
all that I cannot understand—
like why you share choice by going to war
when you seem to control peace
without lowering your standards,
or why you cannot fall in love with me
the way loving you broke my heart.
How losing my head
over the tiny wrongs of passion
has deeply humbled me
with fingers stretched out wide
into the distance that has become 'us'—
because it takes two hands to pray,
because, for whatever reason,
you've offered one of yours to Mr. Right.

I never thought there would come a day
when I would forget to look at every girl
showing me her teeth;
never thought it possible
that I could regret anything
with a promise attached,
or have a reason to accept something
as permanent as a house full of angry kids
and a job to support their hungry habits.
I never thought life could stop
like hospital visiting hours
for those who conscientiously come and go—
yet do not see abandoned mothers still cradling
baby dolls in razor-scarred arms,
or nervous teenagers flattering the nurses
for that extra cigarette break.
I never thought I could be so afraid,
hiding from dogma's rules,
that I'd follow them to lead you here—
follow the seeking gnosis
of a Boston telephone operator
unable to hook the line that circles
the water of longing in tangents
that will not connect but ripple instead,
like snow within the cold
or sex without a partner.
Because poor weather reaps
from the transient conclusions
of absent loves like bad technology
sows the seeds for lust's unrequited entropy.

Compromise Competition

I dreamt of a betrayed friend last night,
her hair almost wet under my umbrella tent.
She talked of a past that never was
and of how much it could have meant.

It stopped pouring as we walked some more—
asked each other questions, confused by married names.
Then affairs broke promises; deceit cheated honesty.
Guilt kept us apart; sorrows showed like picture frames.

Then, crying, I consumed vows in the booming thunder.
Stubbing my toe in the dark, I scattered artificial flowers.
Praying for afterlife company, I canceled her bedridden date
with compromise competition— forgave God in the shower.

Collective Consciousness

(for Joseph Peckham)
I tried to love you with all my heart, but never would you let me
be loved.
I tried to be there when you had left, but never would you let yourself
be loved.
And then I came like the debt of theft, only to find you on Penistone
Crag alone but
not dead.

I remember Catherine Earnshaw, her face painted, her Gothic pale cheeks.
I remember her white dress pressed so perfect I leaned toward her
distant sun.
I remember how she shook her head while her brother watched,
nodded, smiled.
Insatiability suffers for sex to heal.

So I ask again with all my heart: "Will you please remember one
cursed prayer
without delay?"
Remember how Heathcliff cried into the night after Mr. Lockwood
had touched her
frozen hand?
For nothing can heal of *Thrushcross Grange*, not wind to earth, water
to fire, thrill
to fear.

Because lust waits for just the right moment, reinvents the work-in-
progress wheel.
Lust reads too much into the small print of untimely things, ever near
yet never exhausted,
like sexuality connects us with undefined cycles— the denotation of
collective consciousness.
Cathexis causes what catharsis effects.

For all is love without God. All is God without love.

How I tried to love you when you had wed, and yet all I know is this...
that you are still out
there, somewhere.
How by your loving me, I was reborn from dead. Which is why
women and men bleed to seed
carnal reincarnations.
How I have wandered like the Jews, snapped transient suffering by
entropic salvation— married
collective consciousness.

For all you want, women come close to get. All you leave, men go
far to prove.

So I'll see Catherine on the jagged step, show her once again how my
skin blushes against her
heather moors.
So I'll kiss her long dark, receipting neck, fill her snatching, sanctified
hands with pure-profit,
undeserved fulfillment.
So I'll ward off sleep with the bating of breath, steal her soul by the
owning that backtracks snow's commissioned steps.

Still I go to *Wuthering Heights* like a third world goes to a prospering
America,
as you are called back to the drama Merle Oberon failed to capture
beside Sir Laurence Olivier.
Return like Edgar Linton soured to stir in his bed as she lay limp and
smiling in my glowing eyes.
Repent in your darkest hour with the curse of this blessing: "I love
you more than God loves earth!"

Lovers of this world: don't forsake lust nor life's childish ways. All
is enthusiasm without necessity.

Milk and Orange Juice

Something is beautiful
in the milk and orange juice in my glass—
as beautiful as oil and vinegar mixed.

There is a beautiful thing
in the dangerous as well as I see in me.
Yet there is nothing more beautiful
than the Monarch butterfly each spring.

Tell me if you have seen the rainbow,
double-arched on the way home, turning around's
that witness deer crossings in the darkest hour.

There is something beautiful
in every spring, after human nature had told me
to open the blinds and let the sunlight in.

The dog cold air is upon my skin.
I've finished eating a cube steak with red onions,
a glass mixture at my bedside awaits me—
the praying power of death floating by like good-bye's task.
Yet, there is a mixed blood so beautiful I've become glad,
like milk and orange juice, hot pressure against brisk beatings.

She is ringing her hands as the telephone rings. I am forcing myself
to muscle her red blood cells with my white-marriage sells.
When she has gone, my seed will grow strong as D demands bones
thin.
She will fall for shells birds swallow, empregnation's tendered beefs.

One Night in Philadelphia

Jogging down familiar streets,
I can see the city limits.
Shadowboxing with gloved fists,
steam gushes from nose and mouth.

Skipping the steps of Philly,
I surpass the limits of my health
as the morning sky brightens.

I wear this robe,
not out of spite,
but out of the trust gained
by experiences shared with the enemy.

What is it that causes
knees to buckle, minds to overload...
hearts to suffer?

Love is given to protect its fighters.
Yet love, once taken, possesses me,
like this running eases the fear I face
as the neighborhood begins to chant my name.

My war is not just for life,
but for fame's immortality.
Knowing how both imitate each other
is half the battle.

I believe that guilt causes what desire claims.
Anger causes a loss of control.
Hunger is the effect of sharing's gain.

Fear protects my heart
when hope possesses my mind.
For pride pulls my love closer to you as I sprint
down the last straight-away.

Mickey told Rocky what you now tell me
on our last night before the real fight.
I fall asleep to the lessons you speak.
Likeness is the reward of love
and lust's reward difference.
Women make men stable with love
just as they keep them by lust.
Grace heals me through your giving;
entropy heals you through the transience of my taking.

What I'll do depends upon what I know
and what I care about, only you can say.
Still, Apollo will pretend to do what he says
while the media says what I must do.

If failure is the punishment
for every learned lesson of life's cruel ways,
then success is the reward for every dream of kindness.
Life is what happens to you
when you don't forget anything
except the most important thing.
What happens to others when you forget everything
except the most important thing
is what drives determination's fidelity.

For tomorrow they will see both of us
when I beam back at Philly on the TV screen.
"You don't have anything else to say?" they'd ask.

Tonight you are inclusive and I exclusive.
You use me through my desire for gnosis.
I use you by your guilt from longing.

If fear's hunger for success could fulfill you
like my supply of male desire,
then a fighter's anger might be satisfied
by his fulfillment of the demands of female guilt.
Then gnosis might become for longing
what desire becomes to guilt.

It's what Mickey didn't say that keeps me asleep,
as you learn the abstinence that makes my will stronger.

One dream I dream beside you now.
If I could go the distance with Apollo,
I would know the difference one night could make.
Because trust forsakes greed and greed collects trust.

So cry out clear as day my name as I do yours,
when the announcer has claimed Apollo the victor.
Show me how longing's choice
can make passion's gnosis last longer.

There are many women for every man,
yet only one dream for which a man wins his life...
only one night for a man to lose his name.

Chromosome for the Ouroboros Clone

Shawn and I would crouch behind unused school furniture,
like we usually did after our kindergarten lights were turned off:
listening for his mother and my father calls of impatience again.

Their responsible demands became an excuse to heal one another.
She is a young widow. My mother is getting it together.

It was the car accident that had left Shawn fatherless
that would make him befriend me.
I was only absorbing his mother's interest of mine.

Shawn had taught me how to count in fives
while balancing on rolling tires;
how to step on bees without getting stung.

His favorite trick was teaching me to lasso girls.
I would hide in the playhouse during recess,
trailing a rope covered with sand.
Whenever a girl approached,
Shawn would lure them into stepping onto the x-spot,
the place he joked could make them and us into women and men.

Sexual relations have two complementary
yet conflicting tendencies:
one that compromises the loyalty of the mind
by giving up control of the ego
and another that takes possession of the body's trust
by sharing commitment's protection of the conscience.

Guilt is the protective taking of pain
for the angry abuse of trust.
Desire is possession's giving of pleasure
by the hungry use of greed.

The freer desire lets the child ego become,
the more dependent parents are to a guilty conscience.
Separation frees pain by making relationships dependent.
Religion is suffering's vehicle for the ownership of selfish sacrifice.

Some say Christian fidelity is just an ideal story.
Others believe every prophet is an example of moral life.
Some pray for the ouroboric chromosome
to clone the groom's power to wrestle sin with bride.

Only know yin's pull from lust
as the accelerated activity of your mind,
until mental activity flirts with desire's censored awareness.

The angrier desire's vanity makes him get,
the weaker her ego must become.

Only know yang's push from love
as a calming passivity in your body,
until physical passivity blinds us with guilt's naked isolation.

The hungrier guilt's insecurity lets her get,
the stronger his conscience may become.

Pay your dues carefully but in a hurry
while the loss of water concentrates the energy salt creates,
until the halo of emotional entropy floats tears in your eyes.
Noah filled his ark to leave each species the givers and takers of life.

Virtue frees us by taking orders and will depends upon giving them.
What makes girls easy when carded makes patient police hard to bear.

Gossip starts what confusion finishes by mirroring truth with dare.
Though the schism of stubborn sensitivity still shifts my weight,
young beauties no longer play unguarded tricks for the lassoer's claim.

My lasso is now the ink that dries my eyes.
Revised lines on paper continually wash the past from off my face.
I pray the *Lord's Prayer* instead of counting in fives,
mostly while walking in a hurry or by driving my car to borrow time.

Girls approach me from all around and corner me with their presence.
I leave gentle reminders by the way I spread my genetic territory
through the whys instead of the x's that consume rather than copy
life.

My infatuations have become part of the menagerie that once hid me,
like sparks in the dark teach a child marriageable divorce's invisibility.
Love earns fondness by absence but profits from quality time spent.

These days, Shawn and I rave over the fastest score in track and field.
His and my wife come out of the kitchen with trays loaded with
snacks.
Rings slip off our fingers as Lolo Jones skims the tip of her last
hurdle.

Skunking Repression Burlesque

Standing in lined inevitability for elimination's facility,
a hot chick I'm with tells me of her day at the hardware store.

In front of us is a sketch of three butch girls also in a line.
The one on the left is holding hands with the one in the middle.
The one on the right looks to her, confused, a reach like Michelangelo's.
It reads: "You kinda seem like a nut."

"The first problem," she explains, "is that my screw has to be long.
I want one that will go deeper. The other problem is its head has to be big."

My mojo seems to be working again as I notice an even hotter chick
sucking a shake slowly through her chair's raised thighs like porn.

Lust is stupidity's multi-tasking envelop that screws solidarity against nuts.

"What's the point?" I ask of both her story and the poster in front of us.
"Maybe all three of them are nuts," she suggests.

I feel as though we're just cutting bait so I add,
"Love between men or between women represses lust's burlesque
like a skunk."

We do our usual double-take hug as she enters the just vacated restroom.
Only this time is different.
"I'll be *real* fast," she promises.
I wait in front of the occupied door like a dirty car in South Boston's
projects.

Because friends must seize each moment to become compromised
as our passive head possesses pleasures that hunger into angry activity,
until we express the pain that dwells amid love's drowned nakedness.

Sometimes we are like dying tree trunks reaching for air.
Airborne birds land upon our dry branches.
We use the tension of our giving to convince ourselves of abuse's
taking.

Quincy Market bars light our path as sailors flock for girls they'll
soon outgrow.
We finally join hands just like Katie's sketch as we begin the exit
that runs eyes with the walk that lightens the darkness like the comic
of happiness.

Tomato Soup for Breakfast

This afternoon, my father and I eat Vietnamese.
He reminds me of how, ever since my birth, I consume
like a privileged animal— no silver spoon.
I cannot help but listen to his negativity's implosion,
of how my mother met his cousin, a boxer,
son of the brother his father brought with him
to old San Juan to sell merchandise from a suitcase.
How my mother wanted to make him happy,
turn him into a man, rig his fights like wealth from poverty.
How this would-be father had sat so nervously recently,
smoking and drinking Coke despite a liver tumor,
brought about by medications he took less of,
trying to be a better example, behave more like me.
My face blushes with his, we laugh, remember her—
after a New York Puerto Rican joke about asking the American
for "a piece of cake and a glass of milk."
I turn back to my mother's *knight and shining armor*,
imagine how odd his new clean Prius will look, idling there,
as he and I take photos outside her childhood's South Boston projects—
a place of mourning he and I had replaced with the light of another sun,
after MIT turned her *'me'* into *'you'* and my *'she'* into *'Thee'*,
so that he could finally accept the conception that still sneeks up on him,
like one high school graduation shower could become a 50+ dance hour,
until he believed that only she could ever fulfill his needs.
I slobber seafood vermicelli tomato soup with a plastic spoon.
My father wishes he was eating a more affordable, fish sandwich
from a Korea shop he used to frequent after the barber shop
during the mid 70's, when *'The Six Million Dollar Man'* was in,
when her hips used to brush his shoulders, waited like me,
until his inability to keep her thoughts from leaving
his *'father like son, if only's'*, divorce lives from the American dream.
My father and I argue over the mathematics of the Vietnamese tip,
as Latinos break up the ground outside its restaurant,

turn over my family-blood anomaly in their engineer minds like dirt.
He imagines theirs as he begins to plan for his next island visit,
wipes his forehead with a paper napkin he always keeps 'just in case'.
My white tomato soup bowl sits empty beside its 20% impartial calculation.
The owner hopes that I'll never dream of tomato soup for breakfast.
My father's car finally jerks us to a disconnect mind/body stop.
I notice a retired neighbor, jogging in slow motion nearby.
He pretends he cannot see the face he hates because of what she represents.
I look at my dusk reflection in the car's passenger window,
see the orange stains on my white beard, grown to look more like him,
to mirror the philosophy his pity-party high school professor once preached:
"We live and die alone. Life is nothing but complete loneliness... utter misery."
My thoughts go to the woman jogger again. He picks up the mail.
She, like her, is sad to leave him, smiling— mother of my generation's hopes.
Forgive the messenger who tucks you in at night. He wakes with the birds, stains his fingertips with yesterday's news— fencing coffee with his newspaper.

Holy Heaven's Deep

Piecing together fragmented plans like hope's unpredictable weather,
I tell myself to vacate our tomorrows as if mourning could heal grief.
Serving God pleases humanity. Serving oneself hurts insignificant others.
Beauty is shared for love's intelligence; lust controlled for ugly
ignorance.

Mental passivity and activity gives and takes karma for freedom's sake.
Physical passivity and activity receives from given and taken
dependencies.
Her friendship has left me with feared commitment's consumption
heartbreak,
until trust forgives greed like prayer brushes cheating's roots from
wisdom teeth.

Though I treasure the breeze without the embryonic propensities
that connect
soul with mind and heart with body, the way symbiotic perception
becomes marriage,
extremities draw blood for gravitating interests to finally reach us
beneath the tree.
Amen rainbows serendipity as your rolling eyelids open mine to
heaven's holy deep.

My faith may fail to capture the Gospels as you please. Yet this afternoon
swarms me
with His mission like blooming branches are crowded by bees drawn
to mortality's scent.
"One road, one life," I remember the artist sang to me, as I thought
over fame's fifteen.
Breathe and swallow judiciously. For life is but a hiccup sneeze for
teary-eyed laughter.

Brick Shots No More

The air is brisk,
as in his steps beside my drag.
The leaves are crisp.
The sidewalks detour our divide.

It was winter then as we wake now.
It is twenty years later.
Therapeutic scenery still captures human healing,
why we give pleasure for aches and pains to be taken.

I remember how the traffic slowed,
my proud father a signpost, my pace a sign.
I had been overjoyed to stop and go with him.
The numbing cold was helping me to relearn my name.

What born-again would hold his tongue now?
Puppet the prescription regimen, let mother nature win?

I'm still a sore loser when it comes to rejection.
Watch me pick up loose change.
I'm still the poor wooer afraid of sacrifice.
Turnaround jump shots fail to swish distance away.

Hear me sing the rhapsodies that have whipped nets
free from the weight that fakes like premature gravity.

My car, my jacket, my stomach growls: excited by *Taco Bell*.
Like a security blanket, you strip me of my coldest skin.
We have been crossing urban rivers to begin the knowledge
that speeds minds until they brick out shots like carpe diem.

Icicles drip like tears from overloaded branches of snow,
as you crisscross breakfast plates like a magical in sync.
"It's a snow day for the children," you mutter softly.
We sip our coffees and the white space outside to celebrate.

Mushroom Cloud Metamorphosis

"Your love is too good to be good," I remember she had said.
It's not about passion though but rather compromised choice,
I thought as I lowered my voice, measure by measure, till gone.
Because the more chosen passions are controlled and shared,
the harder it is to fall in love with those too weak to be wrong.

I'll take off my socks. I'll roll out of bed once again for baby rocks.
Because I'll make out deep in the night and wake to beat your fear's fight.
I'll keep tender moments safe. I'll talk to the professionals to make it right.
That okay?

After the long tour, I've left behind so much more. This much is for sure.
I see comfort in holding hands, praying together children will listen and not demand.

The voices are silent now. The bird songs have stopped repeating.
The economics of life no longer consumes my interest
nor do the pretty girls wish to copy my genetics.

I sit in a place so warm I neither give nor take,
no longer looking down at the paper
nor up at the light's mushroom cloud metamorphosis.

I'll wash my hands of your desire. I'll drop rope every time you retire hopes.
I'm happy to be hard enough for you until the morning eases bedroom claustrophobia.
I'll cover leftovers tightly. I'll trouble to satisfy your sacrificial clean when broken blues lead astray.

After the long tour, my heart has lost its fascination with the gamble
and the score.
I see security men at work in crowds when the lonely approach fences
like cows.

Yet we cannot be loved by greed's removal of neglect
any more than we can prove love by trusting spoiled children.
Relationships are better off blind to the sociology of soul,
that draws lovers closer by given pleasures and pains
and sustains faith by taking's uneven exchange of them.

I have all that I require... and more.
The children are playing silently somewhere in their space.
My love is always present no matter my age.
Somehow I've seen her in all of this separation
and she brings me more than I can desire.
During her busiest times, my heart suffers not.

I'll listen to your logic. I'll tell you science you'll fail to comprehend.
I hang on your every look when you slang my two-sided arguments
with sexual attitude.
I'll heal the knowledge that separates age. I'll fire synapses with
nervous philosophy.
Induction sways.

After the long tour, I get confused when we're apart. Only together
does our life endure.
I see gorgeous reporters confess, "I do believe he's met his worst and
she his best."

The deeply pleased, suddenly invigorated feeling is earned,
like a car driven by a battery runs better with its oil changed.

Like technology, natural law moves hearts at different speeds
past commitment's point of no return, for the same reason
boys cross lines fathers preach when girls boss by beauty's sleep.

My appetites no longer detract from her beauty.
Every day, I learn to better accept her change's complacency
because of the chain of foolishness she has put our family through.

I get off the toilet with the paper still in my hand.
My great grandchildren giggle outside the nursery glass,
until I, pressing fingers around my ears, squint through glasses to see.

I'll put down my pride. I'll take good measures to give you a fighting
chance.
Yet if you leave me at the door, all the other women will practice
what you preached.
I'll grab you by your waist. I'll dance with your shadow until light
memories awaken dues unpaid.

After the long tour, I've found that *THE* one makes the rich talk
prouder than the poor.
I see no more mean girls up in front, nursing their eyes like the sex
in their trunk.

So don't ask me to earn that which I cannot have. Only don't introduce
me to him.
Because blessings cannot eliminate sin any more than excess can
claim happiness.
Learn to accept what comes in between the trust of a body and the
lust a foolish mind wants tamed.

Because I suffer gladly when you pay dues for putting me on ice.
I feed your ego's infatuation with life by remaining conscientious.
I've learned how to obey love and lust by Q scripture and sacrifice,
burnt candles to gather sinners for the priest's communion of saints.
For the worthy marry by the divorce of satisfaction's pulled punches.

Inclusive Exclusives

TV told me once to walk into the supermarket
only as long as I can until my basket
is overflowing with staple products.
TV told me once to talk with my children
only if I've got something practical to say
after listening to euphemistic editorials.
TV said once not to hide from success
or it would leave stigmatizing messages
on my answering machine.
TV said once to bide my time
as learning from its advice
would somehow interest more viewers.
TV keeps on adopting me
and has made me into a popcorn conversationalist
by making me wait to call during opinion polls.
TV keeps on improvising logic
by synthesizing thesis with antithesis
until I've had to create my own politics.
Because TV always gives itself a chance
to let us seize it by the antenna
when censoring forces us to buy cable or satellite.
TV always moves us with the technology
that lets each generation see the world more realistically
than the previous one just like wide-screen digital
is the insatiable wave of the future.
You see, TV always encourages us to be
watchers with our hearts because it has learned
that, by doing so, our hunger for living
must create a dependence to become its conscience
until we can be freed by an inclusive exclusive.
That's why TV only tells us what we already know
and negotiates over life what news can imitate like art.
That's why TV wants us to listen but prefers to speak.

I guess TV needs the strongest producers to give
and the weakest consumers to take.
I guess TV is more like wine
than an apple from that forbidden tree:
both get sweeter as time goes by,
yet wine keeps us longing for gnosis
while apples leave the Promised Land behind.
Because I'd like to believe that TV is God's soap opera
that keeps asking us to obey souled-out babble
to better understand our own relationships.
I choose to listen to the collective experiences
that teach me, day after day, like group therapy
that those who are getting sick of their lives
can be justified by the negativity pitched on televised trials.
And if TV begins to trouble my conscience
about how power surges could shock my electronics,
I hope at least those smiling actors will ease my inhibitions
with what drug companies say will make me feel better.
Because I've lived long enough to learn
that the more desensitized one becomes by media hype,
the harder it is for TV to cure my peaceful grieving.
I've learned enough to know that self-fulfilling prophesies
won't create hurt but will promote the best rating.

Serpent Power Scaling

Tick-tocking in your grandmother's
rocking chair, I begin to digest
the elevated stories of her past loves.
Driving thoughts into matters I keep,
I shake loose gravitated secrets,
like a dog scatters rain
from fur to claim home's dry territory.

The opaque sky starts pouring down
the heaviness of yesterday
upon the pavement. I sit on the porch,
out of reach of unenlightened selfishness,
and long to be a part of its crying relief.

Falling asleep, my head fills up
with the use of pleasures
that take away painful awareness,
until my body aches awake
by the abuse that empties my heart
of loss and its isolated presence.

Mental activity increases desire's hunger
to take from another's dependence
because of the spirit's longing
for the attraction of yin's pull.

Physical activity increases guilt's anger
to give for another's freedom
because of the flesh's gnosis
from the alienation of yang's push.

Using others makes us dependent
because the used are kept hungry.
Abusing others angers us
because the abused are freed.

I've given into pleasures for passion
and taken pains to get over choices made,
only to find that love has no stake in this.
Our will must surrender to be saved by destiny.
We lose our small space in the world
should we do otherwise.

I stand up prophetically,
release my clasped hands like seeking eyes.
You are master of my dog darkness.
I don't see nor hear the sins you leave
in my faithful heart.
Yet only they can adulate me
when freed from alienation,
as sure as my loyalty
keeps yours running on love,
until we meet the mornings after.
I sip last night's cold coffee
to preserve confusion in my heart
until you return.

The sunlight spits through the mist,
as if the dust of lives long forgotten
could ever be consumed by the light.
We all eventually desire
the content evolution that squeezes
ambivalent freedom into our souls,
like your headlights illuminate my nights
with the ecstatic discovery of my lips
still pleased by the heavens of heat
burning in your eyes.

Because trusting
despite the distance between
only makes the conscience of our company
grow stronger, as your car gives birth
to the woman you've since become.
My eyes mirror your journey's needs
that simplify its destination
with the common greed of a kiss,
as my acceptance
tires you with my vocation's
other departed fidelities.

There lies a bitterness
for every physical activity.
We adopt it out of the fear
that we might become paralyzed
by the sweetness mental activity brings.

I cast my head back in laughter,
my eyes opening to the arrogance
of your wayward glance.
You remind me of
the choices that learn to obey hope.
I embrace your painful doubts
with passion's faith.

We hold onto each other by these
momentary gestures,
no less than calculated pressures
of fingers upon skin
go against the current of flesh
to preserve immortal tension
that agitates the repressed excesses
of antimatter within.
It awakens the spirit with a timeless tease

that keeps salmon skipping upstream,
year after year,
until the seminal place
of their cyclical existence is reached.

I try to balance the cross
of your income's kite
with the tail that lets hearts dance
by the transient trust that once pulled
our bodies higher from life's sharing.
As long as entropic greed pushes
you into the control that drove
my mind to stay on the straight and narrow,
I pray my golden wings will guide you
to my distant Eden.

Your whispers comfort me from the chill
of such long nights.
I've learned to wait in the cool shadows
of your gray porch.
Can love ever forgive those
who let romance heed necessity's calls
while they wait for owed favors to provide
casual sex with its occasion?

I tighten my boots
before its spikes and my taunt rope
around a thick branch and my waist
can help me scale
the trunk of the tree you called me to trim.

I notice the thinner leads, cutting them first,
then tie a lowering rope around
the heavier ones, before freeing the tree of their
unwelcomed weight.

I whistle down at you for you to notice
the nest cradled by the merging
of two lurching branches.
"Leave those two alone!" you boom;
pointing to the dried leaves camouflaging
the frailty of warm eggs.

I give you a thumbs up and finally
descend like an astronaut.
You sign a check
over the hood of your car,
after deciding to raise your charity
to an amount far higher
than the serpent power quote
the job would usually get.
Sawdust sticks to sweat as you
hand me
pieces of our past to grind.

Nantucket Vice

I

Now I know livin' ain't easy;
lovin' ain't hard.
It's tellin' a story
that makes the journey far.
If I've gotten steazy;
if I'm no longer yours,
why do you weigh me down with ice
in the bucket I carry alone to Nantucket
like the lowest common denominator,
my single vice?

From the deviance of my mind,
I discover the reasons you gave me
to embrace my creative faculties,
as if by doing so
I could grow closer to personal truth.

Fire is the exclusion of desire.
Rain is the inclusion of guilt.
Like yin without the exclusion of Sophia;
like yang without the inclusion of Jesus.

Because you were destructive
when I was creative.
Because you were entropic
when I was healing.

Creating for the self destroys desire.
Creating for others destroys guilt.
Like pleasure without the sorrows of lust;
like pain without the joys of love.

For does not your desire still create pleasure
when his pleasure creates guilt?
Because his guilt destroys your pleasure.
Does not his guilt still create pain
when your pain creates desire in him?
Because his desire destroys your pain.
Because women give out guilt like sweat
to race toward their freedom from taking's fate.
Because men take in desire like bets
to create a dependence upon giving's wait.
Remember when it was your pleasure
that destroyed my desire
and your pain that destroyed my guilt?

II

Yet it's not these shores
the water populates
that you have turned away from me.
Perhaps because you too have been there.

For I can see you now on B.U. Beach
gettin' a wicked tan while I,
in aviator shades,
continue to eye the other girls
just beyond reach.

From the dependence of my body,
I uncover the secrets you made into a grave—
to forsake my lust without flowers,
as if by doing so
I could better take my blows like a man.

Fire is the anger of possession.
Rain is the hunger of loneliness.
Like violence without the passion;
like sex without choice.

Because you used biophilia
when I abused alienation.
Because you used homeostasis
when I abused transience.

Freedom is the desire the self takes.
Dependence is the guilt others give.
Like salvation without the gnosis of hurt;
like suffering without the longing to be healed.
I never thought the odds were against us,
that my love would be forsaken by its maker.
But it happened. This much is for certain.
Like death, it went just as it had come—
without warning or premonition.

III
Yes, I know. I should have gotten over you.
Yet I've learned that it's easier to be your servant.
Because unrequited love is the best way to sin.
Because its death is the worst unknown.
For it never returns nor leaves.
It just pushes one into letting go of sharing
whenever the stakes get too high.
It just pulls one into holding onto control
when the thunder booms and the lightning strikes.

For you seem to ride with me now
on the ferry back to Boston waters
while my Nantucket vice prepares

the fusible fission that awaits me,
because hope will seek what fear hides
like give and take.

Yes, you have become the star
that guides me once again as I sip
from a bottle of tea
that sweetens the Nantucket night
as I set my gaze against the city sea.
For your light is both particle and wave—
exclusive as well as inclusive.

From the conformity of my heart,
I free the appetites of temptation's fish
as they brush mine from off my feet,
as if by doing so
I could keep the scales of innocence in balance.

Because you removed longing
when I found gnosis.
Because you removed hunger
when I became angry.
Most times I try to believe
that my punishment keeps me paying my dues
and that kindness is my reward for serving you.
Yet longing for our happiness is like gnosis:
every wicked thought comes from kindness
and no kind deed goes unpunished.

Never did I think that my longing for you
would make you into Sophia and I into Jesus.
Never did I suspect that your hunger
would create greed in me every moment my anger
destroyed our trust like healing destroys hurt.

Yet I'm pleased to say that as a writer,
my greedy deserving is bittersweet:
like true love's conquering of death's unknown;
like the claim to fame brings about poetic justice.
For words, like numbers,
are the minutia of immortality's reckoning.
Their meanings,
like the evolution of possessive identity,
increase the risks for entropic suffering
while decreasing the chances for repressive salvation.

                    IV

For until I,
calculator of meditative lyrics,
no longer return life's counterbalances
of loss and attraction
with the dynamics of poetry,
you will flatter my words like a binary code,
an imitation of human nature, to be sure.

From the freedom of my soul,
I embrace your troubled conscience
and begin to whisper the evolution prayer
that picks the flowers you never gave me
and frees the fish consummation baits.

Because you bless me with pleasure
when I curse pain.
Because you bless me with kindness
when I curse cruelty.

Until I no longer come back from Nantucket
with the blind ambition
to make my bed begin the sound of it,

until I no longer come back with this vice—
you will remain the thrill
that rocks me into good REM-sleep...
the APPLAUSE peaking with my fall,
like the crossing of your legs
could perpetuate the flash of cameras.

Because lust is nothing more than a longing
and love a gnosis for all who know
that sin depends upon pleasure
and prayer upon pain,
whenever loyalty creates frailty
and experience destroys intelligence.
Because possession's happiness will always exist,
even against the odds,
whenever repression's freedom no longer costs.

Because you return possession with love
when I become forsaken by lust.
Because you return repression with pride
when I become forsaken by hate.

And should I return upon your timely arrival,
marvel at how much I've changed
as compared to the acceptance
your separation's literary spirit has left behind.
Should our romance go down in history
with the posthumous fame you've placed in my mind,
take my pain from the loneliness rain befalls those of gain;
give me the power of pleasure desire's fire fails to sustain.

Like returning here could ever bring back
the sentiments I placed in your facial expressions,
even at that very moment
as you waited for "the T"

crackling with sparks along the tracks,
I approaching wearing jeans and pants,
white and black,
only to look past your smile's shy upward glance—
parade a nonexistent future
I had believed my recent letter's response
from your late one
could keep you from lifting into ¨the T¨'s frame,
approach my stubborn avoidance, entreat me into greeting.

Like I could ever watch you save me
like memory to thought,
as if life's door could finally open
and pay the price of art—
like my letter sold with its premature stamp.
As if it could ever squeak clean love's second chances,
believe in the risks that flush friendship's faces red,
as yours had when mine rushed by it
the day of my judgment's Nantucket vice—
always early and never too late.
As if the cafeteria's tea bags and hot water
could make conversation out of a university's fusible fission,
give mercy that extra minute of saturation needed
to drown the weight of desperation with sewing's loose line.

Ex

(for David)

"One of us must be lying"
was all I heard her say
as she picked her laundry up
and slammed shut the door.
Little did I know
that he had once read her the poem
by Edna St. Vincent Millay
that spoke of her entropic frailty
that with every good-bye
silently leads one astray
when they cannot see past the rain
that rolls down the windowpane
and instead read the messages that bead across
the glass like drops of ink that connect us
with what need's concentric web tries to catch.
Little did I think
that, like Edna St. Vincent Millay,
my love too could be replaced
with the hysterical blindness
that has become my imaginary friend
who guides me through the nightmares
that come true in the unknowns of loss
when you begin to respond outside reality's lens.
Little does your former lover know
that I've kept my hands
cleanly folded all afternoon
just because I've been
too frightened to disown them
when someone other than you has forsaken
all but the last of her less familiar possessions
only to have your ex try to justify

my wild eyes by saying something as trite
as "one of us must be lying"
just because she cannot claim
the one part of you I will always carry inside.
For can she defend you better than I used to
when I was the reason
you left for work on time each day?
Can my new stranger threaten me with words
like the ones that would change me like the seasons
when I'd forget to call ahead
just because I needed the guilt of running late?
And yet it is now she who makes me quietly rise
and cross the cold bare floor
with the hope of dawn's first light of day
as I peek through the peephole once again
only to return to the absence of sex
that reminds me how you have made another ex
realize that they too are alone
because hunger makes the mind give
just as anger will let the heart take:
keeping our bodies forever torn by the soul's cost
that, like that poem by Edna St. Vincent Millay,
leaves us all with misery's distant company
and this empty desire to get up and unlock the door.

Mood Zones

There is a temperature
that can make us lovesick.

There is a spontaneous combustion
that will burn lovers like hay.

There is a high blood pressure
that can make us dance.

There is an inevitable freedom
that turns business into play.

Yet there is no temperature
that can stop the heart.

There is no internal pressure
that will calm desire's storm.

For only life's highs and lows
urge us to take acceptable chances.

Only a woman's feigned innocence
can make men into boys.

And there are mood zones
that well up passion within us like sweat.

There are flowers to grow
after choices miss petal targets of regret.

It's the tectonic tension between enemy and bait.
It's the strange alliance that excites us with easy gaits.

You can play tricks and I can make mistakes.
Yet interest hesitates longer than most wait for release.

For happiness is a pregnant choice and endorphin fuel
that passionately monitors the mitosis of acceptable risk.

And pleasure synergies selfish pain into distant virtues
while victory captivates black sheep by near exception.

Which is why freedom turns business into play,
though not even dance can calm desire's storm.

So insecurity, play your play tricks on me
and vanity confuse me with mistakes.

Yet there is no ideal temperature for love,
no endorphin monitor to renew happiness like healing air.

The reason we court each other beyond the flock,
because interest only hesitates in order to be released.

The reason feigned innocence separates man from boy
and mood zones keep strange alliances of high and low

that can pleasure synergies into Einstein distant virtues
and captivate Olympian victories by near exception.

After Passion's Immobile Touch

I don't know how it started, only how we pretend it may end.
First let me tell you what you already know:
I love my future as much as I love my past.

Foresight and hindsight are always present.

In my time... I've seen many fears:
some real, some imagined:
but after the dance,
passion made my life a whole lot better,
having lived more of the immobile hopes only you let me touch.

This much is for certain, as real as land and sea.
Call it wisdom. Name it into sanity.
Your soul provider and you depend upon it.

They are found in the omnipresent.

In my mind... I've seen many loves:
some compulsive, some obsessive:
but after the romance,
choice put me through a whole lot more,
because without challenges there can be no sacrifice.

Because when I'm not quite in this world, painful pleasures awaken.
I don't know how it started, only how we pretend it may end.
Tell others if you must. Remember the storm if you can.

Acceptance lives inside of change.

In my heart... I've seen many troubles:
some simple, some complicated:
but after the storm,
there was a calm only you could give me,
to survive the tears like libido empties eyes of the ego's salt.

Trust in what you embellish, not in what your computer fonts.
Strip emotion down to its core. Build upon brighter days.
All we care about will be threatened. It's love's jealous way.
All we know keeps us longing to be here.

In my soul... I've fallen for many temptations:
some dangerous, some beautiful:
but after passion's immobile touch,
there was something sacred no one but you could take away,
the crowd one gets to know to arrive fashionably early to their bar.

For what is judgment but mercy's measure,
like the melting clock paintings of Salvador Dali?
And if his mustachio truly plucked ideas
from out of the gnostic sky around him,
perhaps air itself is but a surreal imitation of affairs
that fill the gulf of misunderstood loneliness
and turn material quantities into transient qualities.

And yet, your love's healing never comes from touch,
except when you feign drying an elusive eye smudge,
watch waxing wills conscience grace into what is never enough.
And so, you have remained forsaken while my door stays open,
let other minds protect, let them collect your forbidden bargains.
For I believe our surreal chemistry to be real,
as sure as Dali believed in measuring entropic time.
I believe love's healing comes after passion's immobile touch,
the way we adhere to our principles, like love transitions into lust,
allows commonsense to be loved by trust's tender knocking at the door.

Because these nights... I've secretly cried many tears;
laughed out loud to myself from many personal victories.
And yet, mixed feelings have prevented us from sharing any of this,
made you sink beneath the fluidity of influence's uncontrollable rise.
I measure each mile of mercy by your passion's immobile touch,
kiss your every miss like unseen judges sentence your every smile.

I don't know how it started, only how we pretend it may end.
Trust storms into greed for choice to breed passion's immobile touch.

The Passing of Twelve

I'm in the habit of confusing what I have with what I crave.
It has been said that one creates the other and,
like wine to thirst, the more you get, the more you want.

For some reason, this is how I remember our rendezvous—
while I got nowhere fast, you flirted with disaster's dysfunction.

I was not so much challenged by my classes as I was
by my convictions, a power struggle against the sexual drive,
taught by the fundamentalists in a small corner of South Carolina.

From the moment I had laid eyes upon your face, I had seen myself.
I had been so involved with serious destinations, I failed to appreciate
your severe sense of humor. Here I have learned to depreciate it.

For when a half-Italian, half-Puerto Rican angered me into seduction,
I began to lust again— before she too realized my destination was love.

Both you and she would listen to my talk of unresolved childhood issues,
how mother was to blame, paternal damage the emotional baggage
we carry.
Then both betrayed their senior pledges by delivering me into work's
alma mater.

Yet then, your raised eyebrow, strange-tea attention had kept me from
falling's grace.
I chose nothing and lost everything. Now another holds my affections,
walks in place.

Words unspoken by endless confessions have gotten me saved from
that cafeteria,
though many years ago, I would have never learned how to temper
patience with anger,

satisfy hungry risk to create controlled happiness, learn to adopt love to accept intimacy.

It seems to me that in the final analysis, all that matters is to stay the course,
cherish the dreams of emotional attachment, wake each morning to praise the light.

We may travel far and belong outside, yet all hearts remain fixed on the sensitivities
that reveal the deepest of secrets, the power of an honest kiss received and released.
All I want is to give you what you need. All I need is to get from you what you want.
And if we truly want what the other gets, nothing matters more to happiness
than understanding— the passing of twelve that balances the four seasons with sensibility.

I have learned that we must strengthen that which makes us weak, not repress propensity.
For to share expression is to find the mortal spirit within, the flesh that is of one proximity.
Bold sentiments may be sown, yet love reaps frail perplexity— life is but its saved morning.

Playing the Probable Protagonist

Why is a life lived? To be remembered, to be a service to immortality.
It is on those upon which we depend that makes the heart submit.
The elimination of needs is only to make animals into conscious men.

She lives beggar dreams to make me into her player's protagonist,
the panderer of calculated timing, like Charles Laughton's genius.
A director's cut could not depend upon his scrambled-egg probability.

I love her because she loves me. Yet the stability of pride seizes me
like a church creates transience out of entropy, the way angels speak
when air comes back into a soul like an island bares a journey's feet.

If you find yourself looking for a sign in the panther losses that you climb,
look through your inner eye of cool and feel her gaze straighter than a rule.
You'll find her darkness is solitude— your soul her skin's peeling bark tan.

Getting Pissed Never Missed

My brother says he can save me. I say he loves me less than he hates
ash anarchy.
Do you revere church polemics as your company tries to redefine
your profiteering?
Never whistle to yourself when loose secretaries talk to married
businessmen.
Neighbors can be as friendly as cops if you boss incomplete
transactions with dross.

I whip an egg in powdered milk for seedless mornings to pancake
my hangover's flip.
Static air dries my sick sweat with continence as my back is licked
like thawing toast.
Never piss into the wind when store traffic forks your bladder like
silhouetted lightning.
I think I can see injustice now, can stand my saved piss as the man
sits out my profits.

Just yesterday morning, I finished writing what my father gave to the
literary world,
long after nights I would slurp foreign wisdom against his white
noise's drunk TV,
long before he would step away from the madness of boxing mail
before Christmas
just to wear a Panama hat one working night, still pissed over me not
missing cash.

She gives me random customers and treadmill miles. She's the new-
hire romance.
I'm helping her to smile as she counts my cash. I'm praying we'll
both be dead on.
Watch the live media scapegoat smiles as they applaud your long-
awaited recovery.
He answers the house phone as I collapse from last lap laughs, his
stacked domino.

Sacred Fog

What is it that you dream of when nothing but hope guides you home
and reality's suit no longer protects you from Samson's unwoven
thread?
What do you believe in while damage torments those who pray for
the day?

Because God knows you need something sacred like a fog while
crawling for air.
Out of humility, pity, we turn away, as you hammer away the beat
at the reception.
I could try, yet I would fail to cradle your weight, catch you flying
from the top stair.

I walk you to your bed, shaking, as your greatness suffers for my
patronage of good.
He who *had it all* may not be with me, yet remains both here and
there with humanity.
A son is saved by his father so that another generation may learn how
lives are begotten.

Perhaps it is not death, but love itself, that kills us, like a sacred fog
saturates existence,
as we find ourselves in family's sudden grace, still trying to separate
double-vision hatred
from pride's claims. The cross of dependence is so like the unproven
reasons she cares.

Walls, Boxes, and Reimbursed Degrees

I defrost my chilled beer mug
methodically with my right thumb,
seduced by your giggling gossip
of a horoscope history yet to come.
Though docile and dominated,
we remain strangely separated by age—
hardened by the pain that angers
gardened souls and hardens hearts
into the love and lust of cause and effects
that please like hungry sensitivity.

Still, between you and I,
there is a determination,
new walls to box our reimbursed degrees.
You seem to agree, even as her jeans did then,
ever so incrementally— revealing the naked arch
of an evaporating back, sweat rippled down—
like a river's rocks supply and demand attention
by the saturation that bares bones like kinetic skin.

Still, between you and I,
there is a found reciprocity,
lost to the hypocrisy that was once 'us',
after our trust was foolishly taken
by the foreign sailors and harlots,
all too eager to snap the shots that real obsolescence—
the foaming tide that taps shoulders on merchant streets.
"I suppose we could try again,"
I say as you playfully loosen my tie.
Invisibly divisible by stubborn principle,
I cover folded cash with impromptu glass,
make a racket over forgetting my jacket,
and escort you, shivering, her ghost ship almost forsaken—
soul survivor of a captain you have slowly returned from sea.

You order me to observe your virile equilibrium,
as if she could still receive the feelings I send.
I learn to trust the control of your greed instead.
Something about the acorns in your palm,
casino cash tries from squirrels passing by,
tells me the trees profit by the mistakes of wasted tender.
You scatter them as if throwing rice
at chance's broken luck and fate's insatiable loyalty.

Still, I remember her step's bouncing balancing act
that had played her men the way you short complex me—
repress feelings of exit with prohibited entries and labyrinth signs.

"Strolling for four-leaf clovers!" you jest.
Stretching out your arms, you butterfly around me.
"Who's the wishing for?" I charm.
"That's for me to know and for you to find out," you tease.

She becomes more unnatural as you keep home improving me,
wise me up to your religiously hip movements and dietary habits—
the sabbath of perception that aligns appetites like planetary time.
We are only as good as the ones we don't fight the desire to mate with.
Love wages wars for guilt to pass on traits life fails to leave behind.

Still, like her, I rebel: the way toll change had rattled her belly—
offset my heart with her headlight warnings and newborn weight.
Like a jogger's canine, you continue searching the air for her scent,
until I tug and feed your flirting lines the lag they so desperately need.
You listen to my psycho-babble as I finally vacate my wooded eyes,
occupy the muscle in my arm, whistle until joy settles sorrow's debts.

We release from inhibitions like a runner detaches hands from wrists.
Cuddling beside each other on the pier, we trip fingers through our hair.
Wetting tongues, we speak openly, lick laughter's lips of its salty
incognito,
kiss just before skies dusk with mosquito lightning and sober stares.

Dominion Hike Magic

Some drink the wine of solitude,
thinking the grapes have come from the vines of magic.
Some court the weapons of invocation,
thinking that power can cut with the threats of provocation.
Yet we are more than the dominion hike of our inheritance.

For I've walked the aisles of supermarkets to contemplate TV dinners,
shopped for the best bargain variety at *Dunkin' Donuts*.
For marriage is no longer the business of creature comforts anymore.
Company is the provider of provoked solitude.
Its job is to cough whenever the too lonely are apart.

Some wear the sneakers of letting go,
thinking that distance is the friend of an unwelcome past.
Some travel to remote lands,
holding only themselves accountable for their neglect.
I bake bread in a toaster oven and drain pasta in an empty sink,
believing in the body and blood that joins hands like watered fingers.

I turn to observe the neck of her shouldered burdens,
the backpack escaping from them as she grabs for a canteen.
I note the daunting distance between our points of rest and the
summit,
as she takes her shades off to flatten the steamy swamp above her
eyebrows.

For we've come to know a love as fervent as it is frail.
We've seen possession wage wars by the passive departures from
parents.
Submission coughs dominion by activity's peaceful yet hated arrival.

Our dominion lies across the hairs of our forearms
as we crash rocks before descending,
like the chill of air pops dead hearing until accomplishment begins
its work again.
"How are you feeling?" I ask of her pale, stiffened cheeks.
"I'll tell you when I get home," she pauses as headlights pierce the
treetop horizon.

Insatiable Frolic Hesitation

No more do the ghosts say
that your sass snaked into my sentences like a vice just because the
Bible said so,
like when the rain ordered fixed fortunes on every occasion I poured
soy packets over high-priced Chinese lunch special rice like
contagious holy water.

So if you must haplessly go so that I might unconditionally come,
leave the betrayal of parents, the institutions, the séances of
psychology's non-debate.
I only want life to overlap art, compete for the silver and golds of
shared responsibilities.
Like diuretic hydration, monogamous rituals brainwash us into acts
of photogenic grace.
Yet the season of surrender brings the burdens that bomb carts like
foreign corn syrup.

No more do the hosts say
that I pandered my ambition for the luxurious pity parties of fool's
gold demographics.
Yet, though my audience could machine-gun my efforts with buckshot
notoriety,
no one could pluck your eyebrows, shave your crossed legs, open
your motivation mail.

If you wish to know what's going on in my head and in my heart,
all you need do is love me with yours, frolic my insatiable hesitation.
Because sometimes you've got to give all that you've got just to
realize
that you have nothing except that which you gave without getting
back.
Yet the reason you want to love me is to prove to yourself that you can.

No more do the boasts say
that *all is vanity* because men attempt to change a woman's heart by
the passive antimatter
that finds solace from anger by hearing an unholy handyman's Maum
truth at the end of activity:
the wabi sabi of life that inhales hunger's dark matter dust and accepts
forever like dying ash light.

"I have a system!" you insist as cosmetic comforts leave lipstick on
collars like flashed red eyes.
The more active we are, the more barometric pressure saturates
energy with love-lust equilibriums.
Physical activity increases the potential for others to get what you
give, leave what you take.
Mental activity encourages the tendency for them to leave what you
give, get what you take.
We learn to save cake for breakfast when rainy days fail to resolve
blue pain with green pleasures.

No more do the toasts say
that my muse was a love triangle that tainted perception with such
black-and-blue
double standards, only the antithetical could improve the details by
removing the obvious,
mold words into pawns, poems into last rites, books into scold's
shadowboxed Armageddons.

Tornado Dance Infinity

I'm match point playing
for the sting that calls hearts by the hidden strings above
puppet parts.

Consuming makes us
long to conquer the chances that grow old each night with
loaned extinctions.

With guilt's hungry letting go of and desire's angry hold over body
and mind,
you monopolize fleeting moments with funny bone, soccer leg kicks
that fumble boredom with laughter's sweet-and-sour associations.

I'm behaving like an infant,
crying for the energy that warms blood like a mother's milk
soaks sun.

We tell each our secrets,
reveal weak motions that snowball strength into resolution's
holy hearsay.

Some things you return from missing. Some things let go.
Others, like doggy bags, remain after dessert's prearranged surprises
make inside jokes into the happy equivocations of attachment's
humility.

What's forsaken in freedom belongs,
like hopes suddenly lost rediscover marriage in
falling's fear.

I'm sneezing her cold,
shaking hands with the disc jockey's smiling masquerade as we answer
desired requests.

So before each petal of years gone by falls upon *love-me-not* graves,
feather wishes with sappy tear kisses that tether skin like flowered
coral
and take to heart when fermented matters fail to retrieve the
centripetal.

I'm sliding old wedding soles slow
beside a woman I still sway along the party pavement,
lose control.
All that dances
takes on an uncommon air, spins like tornado infinities dry
wet hair.

Sciatic soldiers channel surf every Friday night at oversea bars,
hours apart from the hotel suite in which we heal from *our* injuries,
as if dance were but the shared control that keeps the heart from
hating.

Falling for Kong

In this crowded world
it's easy to pray
just hard to know
how to pray to the one
to whom we should pray:
God judges those
who judge others.
But in this crowded city
I'm climbing
like King Kong on the Empire State.

For when I pray
it's usually to Kong
only meant for me:
Lord knows this full hand
is not my own.
See me smiling
like King Kong beholding his mate.

And in this crowded house
I'm too cold to move
because whatever
doesn't move us
only makes us stronger.
Yet I'm calling
like King Kong beating his chest.

And although pain hurts
and pleasure heals,
prayer supplies
virtue to my conscience
and demands
passion from my ego:

who would have believed
that it's hate's denial
that keeps us holding on
while pressure and peace
are reconciled?
In this crowded room
see me crawling
like King Kong stepping on fists.

So again I pray
for freedom from hate,
that old ambivalent force
that gets things done
only to leave us
feeling like monsters
when we cannot count on
the negativity that it's sprung.
Only with an empty heart I pray.
Fill it up before Kong
makes love's positive crowd run.
Don't look now,
but I've already fallen
like King Kong from the Empire State.

Forget to Stand Still

Like the weight of the week's end,
I find myself returning.
Usually, I take "the T".
This evening, I walk.
It's raining and I'm getting cold.
No umbrella for me.
Sometimes I need to deserve someone.

I'll take you home with greed
when loving's time has come,
until you've no greed left to take you home.

I'll give you my love in trust
when we close our eyes in bed,
until all we have left to see is trust.
Because when loving's time has come,
greed will make you give your love in trust
and confess in fear what hope blindly accepts.

Because you please my senses with creation,
until all you please is what sense creates.

Tonight I'm taking you to see *Ghost*,
after I've had a burger and some onion rings.
I've heard it's about love being
all that you can't leave behind.
Read the reviews, you see.
"Reasons for leaving meet dreams of staying."

I'll push you away with my doubt
when you kiss me on the face of faith,
until I've no doubt left to push you with.

I'll pull you too close with my reason
when your wanting perfumes the room,
until all we have left is reason too close.

Because you hurt my illusions with destruction,
until all the hurt to be destroyed is illusion.
Passing the kosher delis,
I'm reminded of the local beers.
Yet I want my mind clear tonight.
I want to remember how *you* feel,
as I watch you hide your smile
when I open the theater entrance door
and buy you a one-way ticket
out of the week you have lived.
I'll annihilate your hope with my misery
when you lie about what happened other nights,
until I've no hope that misery can annihilate.

I'll spread my fear of losing happiness
when you confess you want commitment,
until all we have left to lose is happiness.

I'll touch you by revealing my pain
when you smile after saying good-bye,
until I've no pain left that my touch can reveal.

I'll surprise you suddenly with my pleasure
when you touch my hand as you draw near,
until all you have left is pleasure's surprise.

You're not the first to lead me on.
It took more courage for you to say it.
As you can guess, I haven't forgotten.
My intentions are good
and you're not just looking.
Together, we make out better than a good time.

I'm coming back with you where I'm now going.
I need my burger and onion rings to comfort me.
Hunger can give a man reasons to leave behind.

This rain has soaked right through me,
as I sit at the Ground Round bar stool and shiver.
Theater lights shining through the window,
I begin to relax to the warmth of the room.
Like the same souls who stop here
at the end of each week,
I mentally save two seats for us later,
just because I need the coffee at the bar
to keep me excited enough to talk
when loving's time has come
for me to lead someone else I care about home,
reminiscent of Patrick Swayze's final line:
"All the love... you get to take it with you."
I find hope in the sentiment,
place some extra cash in the jar of tips,
and walk outside into the neon parking lot.

Sitting down in the lobby of movie posters,
I'm swept by your theater entrance,
and, like the excitement of a fictional love's embrace,
am humbled by the kiss that forgets to stand still.

Because, until the days push us back into ourselves,
we'll have the dreams that perfume a room
while others hope of being the dreams we're near.
Because wave after wave, loves cover like an ocean:
to spray over our rocky past the warmth we seek.

Until, with every new soul's salvation tide,
we bless the empty nights that came and went
before our trust lied and our greed was spent
over such things as coffee, burgers, and onion rings

while we lived blindly by the promises lovers crave...
like the sin a hand pulls back from when touched
or the tears made real when life's ghosts leave lips
slipping with the kiss that forgets to stand still.

Liberation Possession

When I think of you,
I forget to learn from god.
Because I've forgotten
what it is to live.
When I blink at the stars,
I forget to earn the world.
Because every day I see a rainbow.
So give in to give up.
In other words, love!
Because I've forgotten
what it is to live.
When I turn and face you,
I can see the closeness of your smile.
When I burn from looking
at your legs from a distance,
still I can see the joy in your eyes.
Hot blood from heart takes
anger pleasure away from thought.
Because we all get to play the game.
Because from shame's claim
comes claim's blame.
And should we make a date
over the net of science,
don't let me turn to look the other way.
Because in order to give in
we need to take on what he gives.
Because from blame's tame
comes tame's fame.
Cold sweat from soul gives
hunger pain that grows like bone.
Because those who give up
only take in what the world gives.
And if god isn't strong enough

to take you from shame to fame,
remember the ones who tried to love.
If my name should strike a familiar chord,
climb the ladder to my heart.
So give in to give up.
In other words, love!
And maybe if the world's not strong enough,
you just might buy your love a drink,
circle the auditorium of life,
and make a perfect exit
as you stumble to take that last step.
Just maybe you'll give in to give up,
find the possession that comes from liberation
when the world turns to look the other way
and not forget to read the name on your bill,
the one who used to watch the curtain drop
rather than take a chance on love.
The one among millions who believed
in what his worldly mother and father said
because he was afraid to die,
afraid of the honor that Noah gives.
For what does it profit a man to earn the world
from the yearning of another's soul?

Milk Money

I remember it like it was yesterday.
I would hear the news from my father
when the phone rang at my grandmother's house
after stopping by to return a book
that I had borrowed from her shelf.
"Where is she?" he asked.
"Must be at church," I said.
"Gina's pregnant..."
"So soon?"
"Soon enough, I think. Tell her I'm happy for you both."

That's when the fear
I had only guessed at before began.
Hanging up the phone,
I heard a shuffling down the stairs.
TV in one's arms. In the other's, two chairs.
"Where are you going with that?" I questioned.
Startled, one of them said, "We're sorry...
We didn't realize anyone was home."
"I'm calling the cops. So take a seat and don't move
from here if you really care."

"San Juan Police Department," was all I heard
at the other end of the line.
"Get some cops over here right away...
and I don't want to file a report until then," I demanded.
They claimed to be so busy on a Sunday afternoon
that all they could guarantee me was a couple of police
patrolling on motorcycles in the vicinity.
"I don't need your pity trust," I stated. "I get enough
sympathy from my family... and you ain't family."

Just then my aunt with her grandchildren
came parading in through the back door.
"What's the matter?" she asked.
"I caught some burglars trying to take advantage
of the situation," I said.
"Take advantage?" she smiled back at me. "Vamonos,
jovenes! This is no place for children at a time like this..."
It was at that moment that I had realized
that she had also left the door open for them.

No one except me and the cops were left,
save the furniture scattered across the porch.
"Would you like to file a report?"
"It's too late for that now," I muttered. "They're gone."
"Who were they?" they asked.
"Mi casa es su casa!" I chanted as they gave me the eye.

All I know is that, like on that day,
you deserved much more than milk money.
All I know is that giving birth must feel like theft,
especially when it's the family that you do it for.
And when the police finally turned to look the other way,
I prayed that I would remember tomorrow
like you remember every day since then like yesterday.

Pregnancy is like money some people say.
We take it so that others may stay
to face the burdens
siblings bring them from day to day.
For it has been said
that a woman must cling to her man
if he is to remain content.

Yet I believe
that yin and yang dwell

both within and without.
I believe that a woman
must find her own way
in this world of despair and hope.
Because in the end,
we all get milk money
when we forget how to obey
and disobey the lessons love has taught us.

And if we should create another generation
of happiness along the way,
let us count it as a blessing
and not as a curse.
For I have fallen in love with life
only once,
and all of my days have been numbered by it,
like the rain nourishes roots in pots of dirt.

And what of my new family of faith
that has taught me how to live with offspring?
What of their burdens?
All I know is that charity is only as good
as secrets are good at being kept.
All I know is that a man
must receive his woman
if all she receives from him is hurt.

And if children are miracles,
then let them be the ones who say:
"Blessed are the butterflies that fly along the way!"
Because whether man or woman,
adult or child... or even butterfly,
we all get milk money with our wedding cake.

Life breaks those who labor alone.
We should learn instead to accept
that we only grow old
when children must pay our debts:
the guilt that robs dreams of alpha desire.
Longing's together keeps omega's rest.

Sophomore Suite

You would peak the range of my thoughts,
only to startle me with another sly poke.
You could choke me under a fired umbrella,
till temptation flattered me like a dirty joke.

Then trust grew from solitude,
between the stalks of synergy's rye—
when lust transforms fear into energy:
to thrill the soul in an endorphin high.

Should desires emotionally-disconnect like a leaf,
fallen prey to libidinous blight,
you would purge their soiled blades
and, by sheathing them, inaugurate seminal knights.

Memory provides its omphalic meal,
as we say good-bye on the train.
Thorned are dreams: some lived, some lied, most lost.
Tender is that chord's ringing with your name.

No longer bitter-baited, no longer pity-greased:
I leave you this apple of evolutionary Zen.
Calm life's mourning tides with art's sojourning marks—
that from mutation's yolk, I might love again.

Deserve Getting

When faith comes with a grasp,
doubt keeps me pulling at these memories.
But when belief goes without a sign,
grace keeps you pushing other realities.

So if change is what I need,
then why do I still attempt to confide?
If acceptance is all you want,
then what makes surrender's bridge so wide?

For dealing with life's healing alone,
no one can say what love is for.
Still, by letting go... it's strange but true—
everything lost, dreams may later restore.

So should you later hold onto someone,
I hope you'll realize that feelings are sent.
Should you free yourself of what once was,
I trust you'll cherish what heals and not lament.

We've deserved so much... for so long,
that we've forgotten the stories fear told—
when time went by while we stood still:
becoming involved in what never gets old.

What Hearts Get Told

I know not why minds forsake,
only the freedom that comes from what hearts get told.

Sometimes I forget

how children can become our crutches
when their heavens heighten our hells.
Like our love, not even their hearts are alone.

Men are like the games themselves—
they switch between offense and defense.

Women are like illusions—

the lens between what is real
and what men would like to see,
changes with perspective:

like the stories of how children cannot return
the means by which they became another's to own

while never actually leaving the places

from which they first became sold.
Only adults remember how faith straightens out
the doubts that turn like pages when hearts get told.

Ignorance collects and intelligence samples.
Love is the dissection that lives out the limits of both.

Mothers prepare and fathers exhaust

the supper that is created and destroyed by touch,
until their offspring experiment with it for the same
vortex world that spins around what hearts get told.

Now I lie to keep you strong,
as weakness pulls your thoughts into my feelings.

I know not why minds forsake,
only how dependence goes before the call of what hearts get told,
before children take sides, play so rough we explode inside our souls.

Like heaven and hell,
there are but two trees from which thieves and magicians eat.

We slave to avoid the tricks that overcome with the mistakes that
swallow both.

Yin marries yang by taking hate's mental divorce
and replaces pride with the joy of holy happiness.
Lust's spiritual sorrow finds meaning in love's physical longing.

This is how I marry thee.

Calm yourself like elder minds debate issues that make the rest hot
and cold,
professing the chalkboard lies businesses crucify children with when
hearts get told.

Earning Loyalty's High-Octane Hiss

Once there was a kiss I shared with you...
when she was released inside both our eyes,
as she shook her hand gently in mine.

Once there was strife I had to get over...
when I kept her future as your past,
as she looked away from every salvation.

Yet like a two-way speedway,
there are the contemplations of life and death—
a place where people can come and go as they please...
knowing all too well that the smell of oil and gas
can never restore the white noise of churches and hospitals.

Because there are those
who remember closed garages and smoking guns.

Yet there was never a time or place
that I didn't take to make up for my losses...
never went without the life that gave up on me.

Or did it? What are we if not in love?
Have you ever taken advantage of the doctrine:
'The more you know, the more you can care'?
Or could our infidelity be one of unsettled accounts?

Not so, my conscience.
My collar is tighter than ever...
like the *Mazda* you race drives your God to forsake.

Because there are people who believe
that they have climbed the mountaintop...
when even the sunlight cannot make
them do what they really want to do.

Because sometimes endorsements
outweigh the main event
when the *Reggaeton* beat of Puerto Rican streets
revs high-octane engines with salvation's nighttime reawakening.
We race side by side tonight,
defined by the backfire of life's smoking gun—
the love that drains like gutters do rain across rooftop speedways.

People claim to have never seen King
with the women of his dreams,
never seen the friction of a threesome's gain
that teams cost in rubber skin,
screams parables like white noise saves seminal sin,
rushes rebels into sorrows they accept
just to learn the ambition
that spills sunlight like love aims rain across rooftop speedways.

Yet you unshackle me,
help me to become less frantic
with the speedway's cognitive dissonance,
as you rush by my panic in your red *Mazda*'s hush,
firmly shake my shivering God's hand until your tires decelerate.

Your consciousness slows with the twist of resistance,
drop to your knees and beg for loyalty's high-octane hiss
that draws back her adulterated tongue's silent wish—
open the garage door to my suicidal miss...
until energy earns the oil and gas that is never completely burned.

A quarter of a mile in less than ten seconds... widening's wink.

Seminal Closure

The home can become a place to store a scientist's hurtful mathematics—
like a child's red top sets in motion the right to own greed's codependent skin.

When my woman comes home,
she demands the pleasures of pent-up pain,
until her passive sorrows become sudden joy.

It turns out that my seminal closure popcorns her trust into existence,
after her ego massages radiate my blood with the depth of trust's sins,
make me long to release 'for my own sake' her afterlife,
sit real close to her personal ambitions kept public like the media's campfire.

Because it takes a family man to become her soul survivor.
Because frustrations only work when life provides enough information—
like it's better to operate because of snoring than to sleep on a sterilized couch.

No man is immune to another woman's lust nor fully ever able to earn
the mercy that evil gets when a 'perfect woman' judges her self-righteous.

Because I pay her dues, play with her kids, stay up all through the night
when my good causes pain for her evil until they judge them, taking pleasures
in the mercy my good gives unto them— causing pain to she and I both.
She's been my scientist for so long, she's turning into my Hulk fascination tonight.

I sip opaque coffee beside my bedside, look long and hard into the future's sunlight.
Was it a reservation that got the places in our hearts and minds confused?
Is there a breakdown needed to suit altercations to a non-exclusive relationship?

Our bodies are banks of energy. We've taken all nine steps, stripped down our love.
Yet with each subsequent phase we see the other in, we grow a little more involved—
like a kite stretches the dependence of a distant sky by the repressed freedom it's in.

I hear the National Anthem horn its midnight as I step across the stony stairs.
My father has his index finger sleeping over the P.I.P. button of the remote.
Because in the dead of night, it will be she who claims his unforgiving mutated monster,
asks him why he's taken so long to drink— departing from her by his wounded needs.
Though I too am lost amid his green walls of growth, I've seen their two hearts meet.
Will my scientist, like his, finally fall asleep when the notes to this poem are complete?
Can she pave my street with a future that rolls the crisis of night into a peaked ball dream,
tell the birds of our history— unlike the ones corporations use and then pass up for free?

There is a seminal closure when you hear your father tell your mother a joke or mystery.
The scientist of hurtful mathematics becomes originator of underdog philosophies—

like the Hulk she's become shares only part of her day, accepts only night's right to change.

Though my attraction sometimes coils tight, no more do my lines untangle loose and stay.
She flexes thick muscle only to psalm what my mother left me and my father before the calm—
like crushes speak of love's crying game, the onion eyes of boys peeling as greed's top spins.

Lares Vines, Monarch Cries

I can see vineyards carrying turning blame,
see how Monarchs burned Lares Levi age.

I approach her, arms gesturing closure, something about hidden
music.
We drink for dead-end streets, our Cancun.

Love pushes pride like lust pulls hate.
Don Juan, Lino, Francisco, Marcelino.

Can we suffer enough, earn work's congregation?
I preach the San Juan suitcase metamorphosis.

Keep you Cola. *Malta* labors over cheap.
I favor it over burnt fields of sugar cane.

She is sitting on a iron-gate porch, whiskey with coffee.
He keeps calling when she forgets to eat and sleep. She is waiting.

The children kiss her visitor's cheek. He has news of good fortune.
The banks are bankrupt. The retailers have sold-out to the vendors.

"How have you been?" Her caller sits to catch his breath. She gets
up slow, walks away.
Love is the tempest she had tried to suffocate. Alcohol, nicotine, and,
yes, *Malta's*.

How far we must travel, just to read in the newspaper that the bars
are always open.
"Did you come to take me to him?" she asks. He learns how she
confesses to take back.

That old woman is the mother I never knew, that guest my father. I am her mid-life crisis.
Only lies reveal the truth in time that our minds survive like eggs dancing dying-water's boil.

My grandfather Juan told me once that God boxes souls like tantalizing chocolates kill angst.
How much we let ourselves be caged just to fill caterpillar pockets with Cinco de Mayo rank.

Prodigy's Call is Winter's Sin

I woke to the blinding window, fearing the worst.
Prodigal sin is the winter that hears summer's call first.
It was Sunday morning, church seemed far from home.
So I grabbed my *Super 8*, sank my boots into the snow.

It was coming down nice. It was fresh enough to slice.
I trekked the sidewalk to the bakery, heard the crackling ice.
I made history out of my quick-covered tracks, clanged future's bell.
I learned the spells of liquor breath, the whispers of solemn-lived hell.

It's been many years since then. I remember the troubles best in them.
How Washington Street became a Monet field of umbrella-guided
thirst.
If there were but one morning to mourn, it would be on that Sunday
happy,
where heavy flakes canvased poppies with arrogance like overslept
hurt.

Doing Trucks

Babies in neon jumpers, clutching bulk bags of gummy bears.
I'm going through spiritual evolution again.
But it isn't until grandfather reaches Catholic kundalini, open-heart
wonder
that I hear the tune that races up his spine to the last chakra.

Idols bone thin, inventing what's hip– the nightmare of checkmate
surgery.
I'm racing through a hospital, going to a man with arms outstretched.
His grandson's wife cautiously opens the door like a frightened nurse.
He's become the cracked ceiling of my salvation's hurricane-eye
periphery.

Doing trucks with logo stains on company T-shirts as import socks
moved something,
I think of resurrection as a doctor scribbles binary codes on charts;
think of freezing a coroner's smile as he dissects his own disowned
home;
think of *my* plane, carrying my father's resolved delusions to the far
side of the world.

They say every generation wears the same skin, like a calf stands
up again.
I say a man should strive to leave his paternal need for dire cleaning
alone.
But in Puerto Rico, you can't close the curtain between a stubborn
family.
In heaven, you can but count the doubted measures that kept you
against Him.

Rise

"Time to get up!"
my grandmother snaps;
leaving the lights on.
Too bright for me to fall asleep,
I try to remember my dreams.
You know, the ones where
the fullness of your lips
breaks the air with laughter?
Where your splayed hands
iron over jeans around
the curve of your hips?
Yes, it's the dance that makes me rise
with the grounding call
of the rooster next door
that I can hear
despite the cement cinder blocks
that separate the people
in the Commonwealth of Puerto Rico.

For the cloister of mosquitos
have long left their marks
upon my gringo skin.
The night coquis
have stopped repeating
their holy heartbeat song.
I feel the joy of life
enter me through the vendor's van
chanting that catchy, childish tune.
Something about warm bread,
ripe fruit, and green bananas.

"So arise!
Every day is a new day,"

I can remember
the Catholic radio station say
sometime during the night.
Light piercing through me,
I crank open the rusted blinds
and kill the air conditioner
until it comes to a stuttering stop.
The whine of the shower plumbing
prepares me to *'face the music'*,
the rhythm I know I'll find later
down the bricked streets of gold
in the old town of San Juan,
my father's birthplace,
where I'll meet the senorita
with the capped front teeth
and give her family
gossip about the value
of a better education.

I dry my body's eyes
to the sensation of stomach pride
crying from every pore
and dress myself
into my most striking suit:
the man on another horse
that love has made of me.
Clacking my soles
across the tiles,
I turn abruptly from the mirror;
glad just to be alive.

Glad despite the poverty
of an island struggling for choice
yet starving with passion.
Alive with the contagious fever

that catches us unawares
like the beads of sweat
forming across my forehead.
But how strong a weakness,
how rich a greed,
is this bittersweet melody
that keeps calling me to your side
till we share the religion of blood
that lines us up like fools
for the salesmen on the corners
of those golden streets.
Keeps us trying to prove
who we really are
like my grandfather
who came to the pastel balconies
just to escape his boyhood farm.

How can I get
too comfortable in my ways?
For I've come here
to make friends with my enemies
in this fortressed paradise
where they love you
so long as you've got something to give
while they lust for something more,
just enough to make them hate you
when you're left holding your own
as you stare down at your feet.

Lay low and be strong.
For you're just another lizard
crawling in the heat:
bearing the promised opportunities
on your back like a cross,
this naked truth

we call the American dream:
as politicians trade smiles
for the Latino vote
in this paternal matriarch,
land of the wise,
home of the quick,
where money talks louder than poetry.
A place where nothing can ever stop
the sanguine race
for the first light that shines.
An endangered sugar cane place
where salvation is for the aged
and sin for the kind.
A tasty rice and beans,
roasted pork place called Puerto Rico!

Sleepwalk Ingratiation

One foot in front of the other.
Hurt with love pleases like friends becoming lovers.
Ask to recover and carpe diem waits on the ether web.
Task your enemies and weed the living from the dead.
You can tell by the way losses become my gain.

Drinking coffee with sugar and spice.
Making love out of compromises way too nice.
Because I want to share a world that's not bittersweet,
where the good is in *you* and the bad outside of *me*.
You can tell by the way I accept your every blame.

One foot in front of the other,
she bubble wraps me with sleepwalk ingratiations.
I'm passing open doors lining the patient ward,
singing Taylor songs about relatives long since gone.
You can tell by the way I near your distant eyes.

I'll be teaching each of them the means to their end.
I'll be splashing cold water across my face to defend
a truth none of them could explain to my fallen folks
so deep in love with feelings they can't understand.
You can tell by the way I'm reconciled by your lies.

Testimonio is proud yet as lonely as unsung words,
like a *quiet room* crowds a lion to claim his den.
Take crash courses to inherit the meek's seeking.
Grade on curves that stretch marks for the keeping.
What you can't tell is how to reveal the things I choose.

If you want possession more than the rod,
spare her with vows, wake greed with golden nods.
Almost going home, I knew not how to live

within or without, let alone every now and then.
What you can't tell is how I resurrect from inhibition blues.

Look at yourself without, and the world can steal away guilt.
Look at others within, and that same world may control desire.
Yet solipsism only delivers a Docetic womb's value proposition.
We share because forgiveness forsakes the need to bear a cross.
Social justice temporarily parks acceptance before changing gates.

I've prolonged many a branch... turned over every mossy rock.
Still, all I've found is the lust I tried so hard to leave behind.
Wherever there is someone wanting to be loved, lust is there.
Love with lust, and you will learn all that's good in this world.
Your hand opens eyes like flowers speak of solicitation spring.

Solipsistic Doceticism

I'm walking with Dr. King, Mr. Gaye (both father and son), and my third true love.
We're all staring straight ahead.
Our current act of protest will eventually become a topic for conversation
over the Friday night specials of diners for the medicated truckers of America.

Why are we marching, you ask? There are not many who will later follow us.
Yet, unlike the disciples, *all* our leaders will lead one into the hands of the king.
Our words are similar yet less popular. "I love you because you're *not* one of us."
There are much too many unborn to wake the infinite space between motion and rest.

It is a far better cause I go to with them than any I've ever known,
though my resting place I can neither exchange with nor remove from them.
Like the tsunami torrents that scatter kittens from lions, puppies from beasts,
we remain like our shrew ancestors still avoiding daylight, foraging by night.

Who among each generation will fill the pages of each nation's unpublished identity?
I only know what Gautama Buddha knows. Southern revolution is my nationalism.
We fear change because we accept the loves others betray when relationships are made.
Beauty is a state of grand, qualitative danger.

Walking beside each other, our frozen fingers unlock poetry,
as we swoop processed meat samples down our throats
from pedestrians too eager to receive toothpick compliments without
a commission.
We create their need for customer loyalty as we cross waterloo's
succession median.

What is a man should he spread by word of mouth what pagans have
proclaimed
before heresy's forgotten table made solipsistic Doceticism into a
royal justice?
What is pluralistic equality spoken if it cannot singularly shroud a
woman's brain?
For I've heard the rattled longings of midnight that shake the furnace
gates at noon.

The time for closure is always near to accept the resurrection that
exposes living wombs.
Unlike the stomach, they fill without lust's carpe diem nor freed by
pride's compromises.
Because though many may follow *now or never's*, there are some
who seek the change
that heals visions like Martha spoils dreams when men neglect
Magdalene incarnations.

For though I've called and courted her by gestures like the rolling
tide,
all I have are but three words that my other two have helped me to
make into one.
Because though political and musical tastes draw many, an artist's
loves are few.
She reveals her secrets by the smiles I steal from them when she fails
to believe.

Because to earn her hope is to accept the sadness she forsakes
out of the sacrifices sensitivity makes to conquer graves that have
no name.
Because to know how Thomas nailed his beliefs, why Judas hastened
the closing door,
is to know the Trinity that Jesus used to kiss Mary's forehead with
for baptismal birth.

Peter, Paul, or was it Dylan, who asked:
"Where have all the buffalo skins gone?"
Gone to cowboy signatures of closure on exposed film receipts
every one.
Pyramids cannot mummify the Mayan empire nor my Midas touch
make one of three.

G-Spot Exhaustion

I am home. Weighing myself in over a small carpet under a blanket,
my mother waits for me to hit REM-sleep before checking up on me.
Headphones on, I am beached like a whale on the eve of Christmas
with a new caregiver I hear though she is not there. I am twenty-two.

Sometimes closure's flying carpet waits for no one.
Yet while riding it we have all the time required to let its genie
grant us enough prayers for repressed anger to turn hunger
into the straight and narrow guide through the cliffs of ascent.

Sometimes all one needs is to glance, suddenly,
at the private promises lying inside hoping eyes
for a heart to expose everything... as if second thoughts
could no longer hug tightly the fears of inhibition's whispers.

Sometimes startle reflexes create one-way conversations,
whose cop out is the exit that makes pride the first to speak.
Sometimes all we want is to demand that another stand in line,
just to hex the decisions that vex until provisions make us weak.

Abuse alienates by lust's painful evolution to change expectations
for emotions to use the connections pleasure's acceptance attracts.
The needs of the many do much to advance the lots of love and loss,
yet happiness rests in how we invest the brass tacks of one-on-one.

At last, we both caved in while we carried her Christmas tree in.
Somehow we managed to decorate it with the ornaments we bought.
Passively, we reined tinsel; lit the star to signal the kindling of activity:
until we sought the solace of a fire that lingered like water in a trough.

For I am testing the waters; rubbing g-spots for her lamp's exhaustion.
Yesterday becomes tomorrow when all is lacking without her call.
Because if it's in what she mirrors by the smiles you let her feel,
sometimes her missed absence can empty the glasses of filled rooms.

The real disappears when lungs acclimate to hormonal gasoline.
Though fish swim oceans and birds skies, we return to the kitchen.
Hunger comes from love's given pride; anger from lust's taken hate.
Compatible seeds get planted when schemes skip soles like friction.

Framing Gnostic Luck Eden

Mr. Editor, you say politically-correct.
I say everlasting company.
Mr. General Manager, you say shop numbers.
I say trying shoeing the Darwinian rule.
Mr. President, you say terrorism.
I say make America's grass a treatable green.
Mr. Pope, you say shame on the priest.
I say please save the Apostle Judas Iscariot.
Mr. Doctor, you say bite the bullet.
I say try taking this medication.
Because Mr. Editor, while you twisted my words
I transferred ambition and ignorance.
Because Mr. General Manager,
while you laughed at my district numbers
I watched financial experts earn their cool.
Because Mr. President,
while you became your White House dream
I watched poison pills prop like a phoenix.
Because Mr. Pope,
while you changed the church
I saved myself from social insatiability.
And Mr. Doctor,
if you recommend triaged suffering,
then why so few existing patients?
If salvation is in buying off the bully's strategy,
then why did King Kong and Godzilla need a wall?
I say if you want to be great,
you'd better stop trying to damn the good.
Because editors manipulate intent,
general managers respect money,
presidents Hollywood power,
popes bless the underdog,
and doctors impotent need's ambivalence.

And the only means of compromise
is the wind blowing through the trees.
Yes, blessed is the company we keep.
Only be careful not to fall for more.
Because your grave just might fill
with the force of cruise ship cats.
That's what's going on. That's what hisses like mineral water.
And just when you think it's over, it hasn't even begun.
So read my poem Mr. Editor.
Only unload their bullets like a gun.
Pat me on the shoulder Mr. General Manager.
Only make sure my shirt is tucked out.
So get to know my God Mr. President.
Only remember the father and the son alike.
Long for Eden Mr. Pope.
Only keep my gnosis framed like the luck a doctor leaves behind.

Driving Snow Day

It was an untraveled snow day for me
as I listened on my Walkman,
to hear a # 3 Pop song that would never play.

It was my mother's chance to passify him,
like *'Luka'* aggravated his reciprocal non-judgmental way.
I only understood the non-activity of snow's driving day.

It was the beginning of longing for teen mercy mornings,
the start of work's co-dependent listening to a machine
that would magically fail my gnostic journeying for catharsis,
as mother secretly began to shovel his blanketed driveway.

So that when he would return to his white-out, cleaned-error dream,
I would be taken by the collar, cursed for lazy-scheme blasphemies,
as she took in the sacrificial snowflakes she helped him earn his pay.

Mother never had such a driving play as she did that runaway day.
Perhaps she did what both of our fathers refused to let us do as kids,
did what sleep does to chaos, what turns the soil of toil, trouble to
clay.

I was, for her, a victim of accident that morning of heavy innocent
escape,
a hot-tin roof for her motherly foreplay, to make a scientist of
Stella's ape,
cover father's last call some weekday from bars late, speaking
woeing way.

Fried Fish on a Sunday

I've cooked fried fish on a Sunday alone for families gone by.
There was a seedless ease with me those days and the night after
when they burned the midnight oil like my father's bedtime stories
stories hard men church with their eyes, like a religion beaten into
a stolen win.

Do you echo scripture when your wife shakes sense out of and back
into your head,
to service Christian streets where the white dresses sin, where cars
test out shocks?
I've learned to rock like the Jewish pray, learned to stock the casual
slacks that stay.
I cannot speak of it. Yet I've learned of Christmas by moans that
forget their next of kin.

How much this dehumanizes sex. Lust is only equaled by a father's
fine ink, the leaving
of charities that fry fish after drinks, snow you in just because he
wanted Sundays clean.
I cannot speak of it. Still I know the father's stories are the only ones
daughters believe,
the ones that squeeze into jeans, unhook the milk eyes of a lifetime,
its scaled epiphany.

Curling After Joy's REM-Sleep

I live this day
to celebrate the way a man
so beautiful and yet so unloved

walked the streets of San Juan, looking for a simple treat.

A man with something
in his pocket— a comb perhaps—
his hair so perfect.

The wind was listening that day.

There was something
in the air
that made me see beyond yesterday,

like the pasts that come
in the future tomorrows, the curlings
of palindrome seconds and REM-sleep.

I know if my father
were here today,

he would say: "Look into my heart and see the love that is there...
and know that there is but one day."

I live this day
to celebrate the way a man
so beautiful is still so loved.

Desiring one is either loyal or forgetful.

This morning, I am the last and first to wake from this deep
where Kings and common salute with an everyday kiss.
The Coquis are drunk dancing on Meseeh Street.

I am not his Chakra six pence, yet his end is within my means.
There are but two worlds in one— the one that fools and the one that
meets.

See the rum blanket on la mesa. There are three Peters— one petre
principal.
Learn of sorrow's venting. Deny not her guiltless joys.

Shoulder Communion

He says I'll never amount to anything
because I don't think like he does.
He says I've already reached my potential
because he chose the path of least resistance.
He says I'm a deaf mute
because I take his punishment in silence.
He says I'm my mother's son
because it hurts him that we're not a family.

Father under my left arm;
mother under my right,
I sway along the straight and narrow.

I say there's enough hate to kill the world.
So why not call for a diagnosis?
If Judith Wallerstein says it's better
to stick it out than to divorce,
I say let's be dysfunctional together.
Maybe have a baby every time we discover
the flaws that can be improved
if we only experiment with our genetic ways.
We could even make tough love our religion,
force a tear down every face.

Father under my left arm;
mother under my right,
I get confused between purpose and prayer.

She says give god the finger
because he never did nothing for us.
She says shit or get off the pot
because someone else can fill your shoes.
She says nobody's perfect

because I struggle to be me.
She says give credit where credit's due
because it's too hard to take her seriously.

But shoulder to shoulder,
it's easier to believe
that good is greater than evil.
Shoulder to shoulder,
it's easier to believe
that, although progress has its stops,
opportunity keeps coming around again.
For he only says we're stupid
because we have to suffer.
For she says relish what we've got
only because chance blows with the wind.
I say there's enough love to feed the world.
I say it's good to narrow the gap
between the responsibility I neglected
and the cost of doing so
that brought you both to my side.
But shoulder to shoulder,
I know it's the beginning of the end.
Shoulder to shoulder,
I've never been stretched so thin
that the air could wrap around me like skin.

Gray May, Gloom June

So come back with me to the streets I knew...
when love was friendship and lust was more.
Come watch my face become the morning news...
when you slowly wake to remember the night before.

For like Job, I return to her biotic womb just as I came.
Because judgment creates pain's entropy.
Because mercy destroys pleasure's healing.

Good works may not get me to heaven,
but they guarantee I'll rest in her earth's mortal place.
Judgment is, after all, Judas' reason for committing suicide
and mercy only seen by the unbeliever while saying grace.

For like hope, effort, and grace: I am *Father, Son, and Holy Ghost.*
Because lust is witness to hope's spontaneous change.
Because love is blind to fear's gradual acceptance.

And should I visit old girlfriends just to stay pious,
keep your arms forever wrapped around my heart while I stray.
When you're humbled by pity as I become envious,
ask your friends why I write down these words day after day.

For like dating twins, I find trust in a woman's greed.
Because lust gives envy without trust's suffering.
Because love takes pity within greed's happiness.

What can I do for your charity to ever compensate
for the daily routine you make interesting by changing the scenes?
What other personality types can survive the dire straits?
What other kinds of romance smile back like a dentist's clean teeth?

For like May or June in San Diego, my psyche is free.
Because reason saves my mind from anger's polemics.
Because emotion saves my body from hunger's company.

So if I can't love you simply because she loved me,
at least come back with me to the streets I knew...
when love was friendship and lust was more.
If your happiness is merely anger at all the women I knew,
at least let your words forgive me in her biota's mortal place...
when return like Job into her womb's months of clouds.

Because I want to believe in you like the unbeliever
later learns that his hopes, efforts, and grace are one.
Because I need to conceive of trust like a woman's greed
makes men receive their smiles like a dentist's clean teeth.

For what you do for my charity is to change the scenes,
like I try to compensate for acceptance's daily routine
by freeing my psyche day after day with gray's gloom
that lives without anger's polemics or hunger's company.

How I feel about love is the way you feel about me,
when lust gives envy's trust and love takes pity's greed;
when I'd rather be in San Diego with you in May or June.

Bittersweet Synergy

I

I called my sister this past weekend.
You go, girl!
She's now dreaming of starting her own business
and sounded more pleased than ever
to not be paying for the call.
And when I told her about some new poetry,
her voice broke through the silence
when I laughed about having tested new waters
while exploring the corners of my mind.
I care because wherever I go, she finds me there.

I saw my father's old girlfriend recently.
Boy, has she changed!
She's now studying the Gospels
and wears more colorful clothing.
Yet when I told her about poetry,
she became enthusiastic about the life
I *could* lead if only I'd pick up the cross.
I know because whenever she comes, someone's there.

For when I see a woman indulging
with an appetite as sporadic as sneezes
telling me to put down the grocer
because his fruit is too ripe,
I look at her smiling heart
and don't find him there.
I don't bite off a piece too.
Instead, I divide my world of shared blame
into the yang of fear and the yin of hope,
where doubt seeks the giving of hunger's insecurity
and faith hides the taking of anger's vanity.

I saw my mother's latest boyfriend on another holiday.
Boy, is he the same!
He's now a grandfather to another child
and more convinced than ever that he's getting old.
Yet when I told him about poetry,
he became perplexed over my double meanings
and urged my mother to take comfort
in the fact that I was sick.
I'm true because whenever we meet, she's also there.

For when I see a man sweating
in my air-conditioned office
telling me to put something on the table
because I need his business,
I look into his dying eyes
and don't find her there.
I don't hand him my dry handkerchief.
Instead, I let him go on
complaining about my artificial weather,
watching him swim into the danger
that gets deeper as he sees himself
approaching the dry land of beauty's safety.

                    II

So do you wonder why your boss smirks
as you sign for post office fraud?
Does not the guilty customer sweat
as you accept his invalid check?
Injustice is merely the need for greed
when authority spites innocence.

Because sin is never too tempting
for a righteous woman to not pay dues.

Because nature is never so hot
that an honest man can't step outside.

Do demons rid you of the grace to see
how by prayer we find each other there?
Can you remember the true love that led you
to that air-conditioned room,
to the seduction
authority opened your mouth to
as you gulped the rich juice of deviance?

Can you remember how other lovers
joined forces to seize the day
because my time with you
sifted by like the finest sands?

If good is indeed the inclusion of yin,
then why is control subject to temptation?
If evil is truly the exclusion of yang,
then why is sharing more tolerant of sin?

For when your taste in men changes
as the conforming competition frets,
do not your loyalty demons
become the fruits of my labor
as you show me how work reverses
your magical rule?
For it takes frustration to admit
that looking into your smiling heart
and dying eyes
finds every man gambling to be counted
among the few who can learn to live
without the yearning of your good-bye.

III

I got a call from my true love yesterday.
Man, does she sound different!
We joked about how anxious
we were talking again
and lied about the happiness
we wished the other had.

For when I hung up the phone,
I remembered watching the light turn green
when I saw you
driving behind me that previous afternoon.
Because I remember those I never liked
as well as those I could never get over
when old loves create vexations of entropic pain
every time new ones try to destroy
obsession by compulsion.
For to create transient pleasures,
new loves destroy the fixations of longing
old loves make into gnosis.

For when I saw you begin to feel
my reaction staring at you
through my rearview mirror,
you looked forward to the others
that would follow me with my simple plans.
You looked forward to gathering once again
the possessive bellies that trailed behind you
from the umbilical cord of your attraction
as they fed from the energy of your figure,
the way gnostic desire tests a man's courage
until weakness has made monsters out of them.

Because should I look into your smiling heart
and dying eyes
when you pass me over for another,
you'll see a big brother
keeping in touch on his cell phone.
You'll see a boy
in love with the Gospels and colorful clothing.
You'll see a concerned grandfather
to the children not yet born.

For when I rubbernecked your car
through my rearview mirror that afternoon,
did you not see my bittersweet synergy
glow above the slice of sunset
as my heart faded
into the flooding of these stealing eyes
like a rainbow of dusk
as if asking you for your blessing?
When my passion signaled
you to share in the healing of my erotic control,
were you quick to imagine touching *my* skin
when my bittersweet synergy became jaded?
I'm enslaved because whoever I free, they leave me there.

And if I take leave of my senses with you,
know that it's simply so that I might touch
all those who have helped
in keeping my true love alive.
If you should choose to move on in thought
strictly because I've become stubborn with my heart,
know that it's only through
the quixotic possibilities of new love
that I've grown closer to this world,
like words filling the white space of a page
or shadows returning to their bodies at noon.

Tripping Singularity's Hiatus Breaker

There's something that can't be healed or made overcomplicated.
It has to be felt in dual dreams that are always near and never enough.
It happens when the people call, spend their time on your forgetful
fears.

If you turn the page, your world will become but an economic
non-ecology.
Carry her within your soul as she drives ambition, lose your mistaken
identity.
She builds mountains so that you can see the mirage. I wonder if she
sees mine.

Where the people look of fundamental faith, there possession
promises poorer wealth.
Gnostics inform the King to not judge peasant thinking, to show
mercy on fasting blood.
Tell them that will breaks this singular trip, finds love in the hiatus
that can't be stilled.

Spanking Applause

Poets and critics everywhere,
clash your opposing hands
like you meant the world to me.
Because I once thought
that electrons could be bought and sold
like money was mass and the body a hyperon.

Doctors and counselors everywhere,
pick my brain with your neuro-talk utensils
like progress was my punishment and reward.
Because I once rocked
time until it stopped between beat and breath
within my seesaw mind like a spontaneous menopause.

Mothers and fathers everywhere,
raise me on meat and potatoes
like every day was Sunday.
Because I once caught
a glimpse of daybreak's birds singing in the trees
with the light that comes just before the heat.

Problem children and parents everywhere,
rise above prejudice through envy's hierarchy
like we were never left alone to be laughed at.
Because if you want to be better,
you'd better start calling yourselves names
and keep mowing life's grass just because it's there.

Poets and critics everywhere,
tell me how to believe in a god of flame
like only he could make the rain go away.
Because what are poetry readings for, anyway,
but a reason for closed eyes to shine fear on
and spanking applause to combine us with the hope
that trickles from the heart until we reach the last line?

The Last Dance

There was a simple lie
in everything you said
when their platitudes
made you express gratitude.
Listening to you feign happiness
was making me more interested.
I thought I could be a better man
if I told you of the new love I felt.
I never thought that you just didn't care
so long as I had someone else to protect.

I should have guessed
by your pouting lip,
that your marriage to him
was just a game.
Still, you were hotter than the sun
on that summer night;
you were smarter than a rabbi
as you watched me close in on you for our dance.

Your husband was somewhere behind the crowd
when I brushed my right hand across your back
before offering you a drink.

"Just be careful," you had said,
as my brush with danger began with me
telling you that I had found another muse.

Attraction would lead the way,
as you slipped and fell down the stairs
to the bar as the band's final number *'At Last'*
finally gave yourself away.

After midnight,
every night is an opportunity,
or least so it seemed,
as I agreed to play along with your game;
walking you, slowly limping, to a chair.

At the bar,
a man was flirting with the bartender;
begging her to say Lemon Drop Martini,
as I asked her for a drink by the same name.

Handing you the martini,
the hotel manager watched on,
as I applied pressure with an ice bag
to the outstretched limb
a hotel medic was examining.
Smarter than a rabbi, I say.
Only not smart enough to give them your name.
That was my role, you see…
or at least so they would say
the next morning in the elevator,
when I checked out without the date
who left the hotel just after dessert.

Looking at you raise your bridal evening gown
as you sat with your sexy leg propped upon my chair,
I couldn't help but mentally slide my eyes
all the way up your thigh,
as I forgot about the morning meeting she had
or the reason your new husband went to spend
more time with his drunk, garter friends.

Now my new family members
asked us to play the same game,
as they suggested that I take you to your room.

Yet adultery is not only a woman's game,
to make an old friend into a jealous enemy
and a second cousin refuse to play by spouse rules.

And because rules are meant to be broken,
I tried in vain to resist temptation,
as you began to sip from your martini.

"He tries…" you would say.
To win my trust, you would have to put me in between.

Until, seeing the groom in me take over,
you apologize for your lie and get up to dance,
as the words to our song still play somewhere
between our hearts and the back of our minds…

"I've been climbing hills from my past,
only to realize that life is as flat
as a lake below love's mountain surpassed.
All its rivers descend down the same path
whose answer is but a question we've asked
when we prayed for gravity's harmony at last.

We may call it cautious or too rash.
Yet here it is… putting us both to the task
of placing greed somewhere else to be had
when love divorces us of its envy at last.

Looking down the guest list, you gasp
at how many witnessed the vows we cast.
They wait to hear how we'll spend our cash
when we uncling on the honeymoon at last.
The band plays our song, the lights fade in class.
We remember the tears that cried like mad
as slow affection met feared rejection too fast

the first time we danced like children parents grasp:
cradled by the dependence love's freedom lacks:
when gallantry pulls you into my arms at last."

It's true. I've searched for true loves after adolescence...
only until they could lead me to my first flirt with you
and the perpetual dance with antipodes
that keeps relations with the opposite sex elusively new.
It's also true that nothing ever happened between us,
like the family bet made long ago
that you could teach me infidelity
ended with the test of us going to the bar that night
after echoes from *'At Last'* made you say,
"You'll always be the smartest guy I never married."

How I changed my tune after our last dance
across the bar floor I may never know.
All I know... all I have of you is our song.
Yes, I have changed my tune,
like the faked injury from that night could save me
from the ones that now try to make me stay home.
Soon all will learn how my fidelity won the family bet.

Until the groom smiled back at me,
I hadn't realized that he was,
and had always been, my muse.
My looking for another one was only your doing.

He remained apart from us
only long enough to give us the last dance,
as you reminded me of the lines to *'At Last'*
the bridesmaids and groomsmen at the bar
began to sing to us...

"Lovers may get old and tired,
yet more love is given than is required."

Clinking our glasses gently together,
the groom and I raised them to the heavens,
as you winked at me one last time.

QVC Sells The Lid Tick Red Carpet

A hair in the eye needs a good tear to flush.

I think the Man who Buster Keeton-ed me
in the silent theatre deserves a wack in the face.
But who am I to disagree with the Kirk's
of bad technology
or the perks of poor weather?
The hardest part of lateral transition is healing the HR spot.

I guess Father was right.
There is no cure for the early curves.

My house is getting soft,
like frosted flakes in a bowl of thoughts.

Tiffany Haddish slaps Richard Gere
on the back of his free hand at a movie premiere,
as Pretty Woman enters wearing my Oscar dress,
that red one I got from QVC on a one-night stand
with vertigo stairs and Pretty Woman smiles.

My cell phone battery flatlines
like an open-house hurricane Dead End bar.

I 'wanna go back' like Eddie Money.
I really need to get it wrong just for fun.
My needs are less so I give more.
So "give and take" music over the bridge of deer
'getting the big hit' of cracked windows,
spill milk on your kitchen floor without regret,
stay sharp with your beer bottle glass,
keep everything from getting spoiled.

I've really missed you.
Got to go.
I'll pay you as soon as you can.
Film me on vibrate.
The rub of trust is selling-out a real girl on your most vacant part.

I want your QVC salt as I slip deeper into the bathtub, leave you at last.
To see you, head down like that, makes me sad.
I've come to know your gradual dusk again.
Unlike Paul McCartney's song, all I have are lonely nights.
They save me from desired guilt and help to destroy another man's reality.

II. <u>No Sky Should Zone Ambivalence:</u>

"Your father can't help you anymore."

The Missing Hour

You will not return this prayer when you come to lay beside her,
speak to B-line's holy brave, summarize to all what you've saved.
We learn to compensate when the world favors dreams to sleep.

I was the hidden seeker of your venting ex's unforgiving needs.
You pleaded denial when I saw laughter in your suffering eyes.
She was the fire you never lacked, your resolution's missing hour.

It comes to some in the repressed release of forbidden thoughts.
Some speak to distant relatives in the flavors of sleep long lost.
I was humbled smarter by the shared desserts of sandman desires.

I got arrogant the harder you pushed, dumber the more she pulled.
She would eventually kneel to your meager self, her devoured trust.
It's hard to please hurt when ill profits from counterbalanced greed.

Lack of use creates intelligence. This increases intolerance.
Absent abuse encourages ignorance. Presence creates use.
Use creates arrogance; arrogance ignorance. Abuse envies pride.

You can't steal salvation by murdering ego any more than ego can
steal charity by murdering compromise. Seize guilt's sacrificial son.
A woman is only impartial to sloth laborers, impotence's childless cow.

Will draws hope from within. Grace calls upon drought to forsake
fear.
It is but the missing hour that we desire, a chance to work it out
alone—
feel her adrenal lie crisis her inconvenience, marry the easily amused.

When You Have Love

When you have love,
your father hides the silver spoon and the post master
seeks the posthumous noon.

When you have love,
the newspaper goes unread and old letters
stir in your head.

When you have love,
the close family divides while on vacation and children
play secret games instead.

When you have love,
there is the distant calling of the shore and fishermen
cast their lines out much further.

When you have love,
girls use girls and boys abuse boys
over the tricks of jam buttered bread.

When you have love,
the wall clock ticks as the sunlight
pushes dust over the windowsill.

When you have love,
Christians reclaim hope and Cervantes
charges fear like impossible dope.

When you have love,
you learn more than you thought you knew,
rejoice in having nothing.

When you have love,
there is happiness in suffering and selfishness in
sacrifices never claimed.

When you have love,
there are only the two of you— dry baptized laundry
for the tears you've made of laughter's heavenly abode.
When you have love,
the world competes for arrogance and sensitivity just because
love and lust can neither be proved nor removed.

When you have love,
your grandmother fills the silver spoon and the manufacturer
cures bacon from farms starving for posthumous noon—
when you have love.

Love and the Media Equity Pitch

I didn't know
that you would charm me after letting me watch you go,
like a newborn in an ex's arms.
I didn't show
so that you could come back to my honesty like a lie
of secrets better lived alone.

Yet you listen faraway
as I undergo the lover's change,
watch tears fall from truths jealous others claim,
see them stream down eyes like melting sky windows.

And so I compose for you this Valentine Day's score,
the music that screams for you outside your door
with the promises that cut stems
until petals open with the love that dies forever slow.

Because I'm happiest when you reveal your scent...
sad to breathe in and out alone.
Lies are hatred's fermented odor—
the bite of charm that turns apple spice into foreign wines.

How little we know of its tomorrows though...
the paying of marital ways.
How we suffer gladly nobody knows.
We show only for the lover's change—
the staying power that stretches conscience clean
with the insurance that hugs us into letting go
of the perpetual seeds Mama plants in adolescent dreams
when media pitches its mojo equities.

For there are values I long to sow
in the immature soils nymphs never outgrow.
There are honesties I give to let you know
the realities that reap sacrificial tweets
despite the illusions that sweeten responsibility's show.

Because I didn't know
that you wanted others to wonder who loved who so—
warm their lies with intentions that melt feelings like an invisible glow.
I am the window that refuses to close,
the 'yes' that never learns to say 'no',
keeps believing promises better lived alone—
the cut stems still closing petals like a newborn in an ex's arms,
proclaiming the secrets we may never know,
the scent of happiness that ferments lies into apple wine charm.

What is a Man

There is a man
who cuts the trees, screams at the skies—
amputated from the world.

There is a man
who buys potatoes for those who cannot eat them
after all the menial work is done.

There is a man
who fails to answer the Doctor's orders,
lies to him about the children he never knew.

There is a man
who looks into the woman's eyes,
tells her he loves her and desires to compromise.

There is a man
who profits the bank with summer assurances,
feeds them taxes to insulate them through the winters.

There is a man
who spreads the company stock to strangers,
runs innocent people from the streets businesses curtail.

There is a man
who listens to the sawing of trees
that imbalance ringed fingers upon an earth married to heaven.

There is a man
who loves a woman for who she is,
asks to how to satisfy her endless needs, time and time again.

What is a man
if he is to be half as strong as a weak woman—
the atmospheric Armageddon that swallows planets with red sun air?

Eve's Dropping

I would double guess humor and she would scream:
"To live with cuddles is to divorce my company!"
Now she libraries lunar landings of four sense dreams,
until I shake in puddles like birds, wake to REM-sleep.

There is a man who wrestles in his head.
There is a woman who bleeds for his kin.
I awake this morning to rain falling dead,
as thoughts are pinned like clouds on tin.

To reporter who freed an artist to speak his mind,
the documentary film made more money than news.
For the fans, the song spoke louder than the words.
Still, it was the drop of hard life that made him easy.

We swallow more to need less, make peace over war.
We take leaps of faith before falling on our shared truths.
Pride goes before love because hate is self-destructed lust,
until others get crazy over kindness, can never give enough.

I lay in the quiet dark, a periodic crack of light from closed door
tells me my true love has learned I died fighting to get over loss.
I breathe nurse sorrows as they slow my headlight past, warn to
walk the morning hall fast, interrupt calls with immigration costs.

The spider builds her bridges to trap, a fly bounces walls of poor escape.
No one asked for the duet escapades that beat the bank with fool's gold.
I was told to lie so that she could betray— gave Motown my rainy
sun day.
Some people stay to leave the family lot. We pray they won't lose control.

Waiting for Marmalade

She liked me to jar my marmalade lips against hers right,
as she covered my face with her French-gloved hands.
I'd turn the house door lock with her regally-earned might,
fill wealth with pins for strings of clothes-line, communion cans.

She biked with me on Christmas cliffs spent together in France,
told me how to demand wine while inspiring acceptable grace.
She'd burn butter for my scrambled eggs and morning paper,
as I believed she folded the cards I played for Mary's missing ace.

She wore shoe-box heels and see-through lingerie. Her hair curled,
she kept me safe, spoiled my lies with shared silences, handkerchiefs
ironed out, took me down surrender's stretch of money, waited to twirl
as I learned to turntable roots, tabernacle trees with regenerative leafs.

Kundalini's Karma Resurrection

Sober now, I wake to supper and sleep with you after confessing my heart.
Insecurity only wants what it can't have, vanity to have what it doesn't
want.
The neglected only hunger for what the spoiled anger for: being alone
together.
The rain begins as we each make breaks to our cars. No more tailgate
directions.
To witness your headlight's raw approach is to ripen expectations
like mangos.

So come closer to the cabala eyes you've made for me to desire yours,
as karma's *Second Coming* stirs kundalini's cauldron like water in a well.
Listen to prenatal humming that echoes our panting's palindrome mingling,
as we lose the small change that exchanges faith's given for doubt's taken.
You do what I like. I remember what you forget. Love excess is what
we lack.

We remain loyal to the fight that keeps the proud walking a tightrope
of light
just like a golfer swings his clubs to follow an imaginary line to
distant holes,
as we better understand the determination that fails to clothe
obsolescence.
Sold on blind currents that charcoal glow comfort within rubber
band holds,
we only stop after calories empty and digest slow as a homemade
sandwich.

Woman Measure Man

One man measure heart with mind.
One man divorce 'no' by 'yes'.
One man require more because she desire.
One man satisfy guilt by needing less.

One man measure by the home he lost—
the harder he come, the more she test.
One man find a God in him through her love.
One man search Bible to parable quest.

One man grow in a world alone—
learn to surround wealth with technology.
One man visit parent with gallon of milk—
eat sugar flake and *Velveeta* cheese.

There is but one measure for every man
to kill the parts of genes yet to be whole.
Woman give her man enough time to kill,
because to live with is to live alone.

Agitation creates hatred, hatred self-love.
Self-love creates hatred out of pride.
Pride creates lust out of greed,
greed trust by the unknown.

One man come to write of love.
One man marry 'yes' to 'no'.
One man divide mind with heart.
One man die to know.

Tea Time

I've grown tired, old friend— too tired to stroll these streets again.
I've grown sick of their monuments and all the names you knew so
well.
Take me away from our two months of Beantown, after-class talk.
Take me up our winding stalk, to pierce your fallen earth with my sky.

I don't remember when I started to forget what began those many
years ago.
Still, I've come to lose a part of myself, that pulse that had once
belonged to us.
I don't know when I first let your darkness enter my soul, how my
optimism was
sucked dry by the hurt of sudden memories, to leave me shuffling
back alone.

For when I try to say good-bye, still you answer my pride with a
frown,
pretend you never cared much for poetry, how it only keeps you from
being
what you want to be, makes you lie about what was, the way it could
have been.
I bask in the glow of desire's recollected sun— ask where these blues
come from.

Yet until there comes a day that you may surface my passion's
stalagmite sea,
I will keep on walking. For even old times can heal wounds, the quiet
possession
of those who walk among the shadows that dance for all who can
hear the music.
In my darkest hour, still you silhouette me with your black tangled hair,
heighten sex.

I had the same old vision again last night, the one in which the white bearded man
tells me of his Exodus parable from the valley of education to the mountain of pride.
He enlightens me with his triangle of light, the one ionic surges create out of might—
peaks a covered head and legs with Christ's camel, passes through rope's needle.

This beggar had turned to thief when he came to love a woman more than himself.
He again led me to her God's ruins deep in the green, told me of her sisterly grace.
Again, he tried to swallow up my thoughts as sunlight blinded his bloodshot eyes,
drank as my spiral stairs touched a love his crawling heart-vines had failed to reach.

For now it begins to rain as I try to say good-bye to this God forsaken place,
avoid wanting to greet the mysterious stranger that meets me at ¨the T´s¨ stop.
He doesn't smile back, knowing that I too am alone by the length of my stare.
Loss has helped me to accept this cold, fluttering through his push-pull clothes.

No, dear friend— I won't search down your broken-promise streets again:
my mind half-owned; my body cold-wet. The voices now call me by name.
I tell me the time has come for me to believe in love's better place:
where compulsive obsession finds identity; where the streets are gold.

Schizophrenic Spiral

(The Surgeon General has warned that reading this poem may
be hazardous to your health)

No person is indispensable:

I could have looked deep into your eyes as I sighed.
But it was in your nature to avoid letting me confess.

There's safety in numbers.

He's off the wagon again:

I could have left you worried over getting married.
But it was in your nature not to let me hang to dry.

There's no such thing as a free ride.

Get that monkey off your back:

I could have told you lies and left you with nothing.
But it was in your nature not to make yourself say "please wait".

There's no substitute for victory.

He just got out:

I could have called you to open my closed cage of selfish tears.
But it was in your nature to provide me with the chances that
futures cry.

No one is above the law.

Actors take your places:

I could have spoken out of turn about the part you'd play.
But it was in your nature to pace hearts down their own unpaved roads.

There's no business like show business.

The light's on but there's nobody at home:
I could have loved you more just in a ¨no¨.
But it was in your nature to boycott sirens with forgetting's gradual ¨good-bye¨.

Close but no cigar.

It's not you, it's me.

I could have changed my mind, drowned water with wind and earth with stars.
But it was in your nature to fly forever, never accepting infidelity's nine months.
Life is spontaneous combustion, applauding conflict with confusion's pause.

Casper's Summer Ghost

I was driving in my car
and the camp wasn't too far,
but my son was crying
telling me not to smile all the while,
I know not why.

He was walking in the crowd
and everybody laughed out so loud,
but he wore that mask so darn proud.
They called him Casper,
and he cared for all of them somehow.

Another's mother had believed
in giving his face reality.
Then he just looked in the mirror
and said, "Me, me.
That's my face and I will wear it,
like the birds and the bees."

He wonders where is his soul.
If it creeps and hides somewhere
beneath his pillow.
Yet every elementary bully knows him
as 'Casper, the Friendly Ghost',
though they walk so bold.

Every other life brings a scapegoat
who learns the strife
of how black and whites
never fit quite right.
We ask of others what we ourselves don't want,
wrong or right.

But in the end, we all love,
and this living is only answered up above.
So take off your mask and say you'll not
question the things she does for you,
and she'll wear your ring like a mask,
just because.

Fond Memories

I recall a person I once knew,
her memory full of pretty scents.
She reminded me of a past that never was
and of how much it would have meant.

I remember the joy she gave to me
and all the moments she turned to gold.
Yet time goes on and I stand still
and instead think back of good times now old.

I've traveled so far to return with pain;
searching for a meaning I've wanted so much.
Yet now I know I could never understand.
For the answer lied within her touch.

Hermaphroditic Hierarchy Rite

Sometimes

you never know
when it's gonna come
whether it's a virgin or the worst kind.

I looked in the mirror

sometimes

wondering if
I'm the one,
forgetting all at once
why you left me here.

Yet then
I see the motion
like an invisibility calling me—
forget to leave all
my belongings behind.

Sometimes

you want a sanctified lay
to remember
the reason you're here,
because we only act
when others have it too bad
or us too good.

Sometimes

all that matters
is the sunshine that keeps the rain of fear.

Because when I look out the window,
I can't see past myself,
the way you used to see me.

Because

sometimes

all you've sent and received
are googles of oozed actualities
for word of mouth to become
a natural law
for those who have it too good.

Sometimes

this life weakens dreams,
like lies strengthen art's holy architecture—
change my understanding of lust and love
as if their hierarchy were but a hermaphroditic rite.

Sometimes,

I forget
why I'm here—
only try to remember
the remaining riddles instead.

And yet still you make me
wonder
through imitation's
'nevermore's'

if I could always keep you near...
perpetuate a puzzled pieced sense
that allows ideal needs between ideas
to fit just right.

I know not how thick
the mirrored glass,
how many false loves we must break
before a man can learn to please his wife.

All I know
is that we have learned to live
within a
synchronicity
as momentous as the
daybreak
between yesterday and today,
when the past is chased by tomorrow.

Because I want you
like that very instant,
like love in the Bible sense of the word...
want you to keep my safe,
read to me this poem
just before and after I wake,
like only it could tell us the things
our words have all but failed to convey.
Because the deeper in love one gets,
the easier it becomes to not do what words say
and feed from hidden feelings sought and left behind.
Because sometimes we meet in between laughter's love
and lusted after sorrow, dart at sex like poisoned arrow tips,
penetrate the lips that seethe nostrils with venomous grace.

Solitary Sunday

If I could stop the frames racing with your glowing face in my mind,
I'd keep them on a shelf in my memory's virtual occupancy library:
to access electronically in every disconnected place, at any given time.

As long as we can bother our heavenly father,
we'll have circumstances to keep us making the right choices.
Until faith's will on earth grows too old to give birth,
righteousness will be tolerated by the tide of unswallowed voices.

Because despite the temptations solitary time brings from strangers,
you rob them of the treasures they hide within trust's secret gardens.
Because I borrow from your beauty every time I escape the dangers.

If your heart muscled mine with questions of infidelity's wrongs,
I'd protect your doubts with my bones and pray before answering:
until shadows stretched across your ceiling to greet you like dawn.

We sensor the sexual while praising God for perpetuating the species.
Physical activity loses its focus from the alienation of guilt's
confusion.
Mental activity is attracted to the supper that gathers desired energies.

So give us this Sunday, without the fellowship of a sermon's cure,
to remember the sacred falling for greed's daily bread.
Forgive us our debts as we forgive our debtors,
and let trust warm us like a blanket clothes the skin of a bed.

Until dietary desire raises my internal temperature like good dreams
pacify guilt by hunger and sleep retires anger from its daily exercise,
mornings will beard floors that bounce revelations like trampolines.

For love cannot justify all of life's personal glories,
though joined at the hips we as humans are.
Only because cruel smiles sever from clever lips pride's untold furies,
do children break the rules of adults by going too far.

Beauty and the Beast

She walks like a cat
whenever I let her go
all the way back home—
though I can hear her
purring for me to follow.

Turning around,
I catch a glimpse of what
I gave up for this
and a part of me aches
just to think
that she feels it too.

It's the same
the next evening—
only this time heels
somehow make
the moment click
and I find myself calling
for her to come back.
Laughing, she blows
me a kiss
I catch with my heart.

And that's how it began.
I caught. She kissed.
Daydreaming at night,
I hardly ever went to sleep.

Every morning I longed
for her to return the favors
I couldn't bear to let lie.
Then there were the calls

telling me she would be late.
Another party.
Another rendezvous.
Before long,
I was calling her.
Only I was always early.
That's when the makeup
started to get to me.
It was as if I wanted
her to dress up for me
and not for the crowd.
I wanted a sanctified lady!

It wasn't long before
we were friends.
Coffee at midnight
became dinner at eight.
Soon I was wearing ties
to her dresses
bought with overtime pay.

We were steady,
on the way to 'better things'
when out of the blue
she tells me
I had knocked on her door
one too many times.

But that was nine months ago.
Now she's happy and I'm relieved.
Beasts come from the tomorrow hurts
of beauties with no feelings to show.

For better or worse,
we've separated.

For richer or poorer,
we pay our own way.
In sickness and health,
my mother either can't stand her
or just doesn't give a damn.

So I e-mailed her today
and told her I missed
the casual good-byes
when she walked like a cat—
told her not to purr
without an excuse.
I don't expect
she'll e-mail me back.
You see, it's been an hour
and I've got it in my head
that she's going to leave me
for another cat.

Just for her,
I'd change my web address,
change my account name...
do just about anything
to receive her actualities—
anything to not stay her dog good-bye.

Penultimate Precipitance

You stepped so gently up my stairs,
I felt like the slinky anti-gravity moves.
And when our night was over,
I spent all morning thinking of you.

Tall have become our memories.
Short good-byes we know.
Desire overflows like a river.
Its banks of guilt no longer hold.

So if I tell you, "I feel alright,"
kiss me once and I'll kiss you twice.

Forgiveness gives us all the answers
while the others fall under seduction's spell.
No questions to ponder.
Our discoveries are the whispers they yell.

It's about a parent calling one naïve
after we've been swallowed whole
by being kissed once... then by kissing twofold.

There are ways back into loving:
taxis heading downtown, coastal trains.
They all take us to that *'someday
we'll be in each other's arms again'.*

You were 18 years old then:
that legal age of innocent beauty.
They said you made me feel younger.
Maturity is, after all, the human law of relativity.

I'm a *'one-woman man'* now:
learned to be exclusive with my head.
Yet you've become a *'no-man woman'*
who'll only forgive me once you're wed.

Love and lust are lost and gained,
like a binary code of *on* and *off*
gives trust to yin and greed to yang.
Forgive me for the worst of sins: scoff.

Trespassing lips is only forbidden
to those who second without getting to first.
We kiss sweetly... then kiss again with passion's thirst.

You turn my car radio to your favorite station.
We lean close to inspect the passenger floor.
You place your hand upon my knee.
I cover it with mine and close the door.

On the edge of our seats, baited breath fogs windows,
so quickly raised that swans dip their heads
into the nearby lake as fingers squeak glass with sweat.
Our volunteered vows pass ambiguous ambivalence's test.
The purple skies pelt my car's roof with wizard rain.

The motel signs read *'No Vacancy'*. We pretend to harass loss,
like ice cream melts split promises with banana sprinkled trash.
I brush back your bangs, unveil your burning eyes
until smiles speak love into existence, peak penultimate precipitance.

We've waited for this moment for so long,
that lovemaking has given dreams sexuality's sound.
Because despite acceptance's two directions of changing,
caring for each other keeps intimate feelings around.

I would much rather fly,
though I stumble to stay humble.
Kiss me softly and I'll kiss you double.

So here's the ending
to this fairy tale once an open mouth had begun.
Like bread crumbs, we learn to follow
the trails that make relationship's work into fun.

Still, it's in our nature to consummate
our every *what if* with each forever 'I do'.
It's in every card we take to play
and in how belief tells us the good news.

Yet should lies task us
to not kid ourselves by asking:
"Do I *still* please you?"
Kiss me once and bid me twice the chance to obey.

For eyes are only tranced by tears of grace and entropy
when we choose to be ruled by parental scoff.
Grace mothers *'more or less';* entropy fathers *'never enough'.*

Tell Me a Little Truth

There was a white lie
in every joke they said
and in every tear you cried
when my listening to your truth
made me ask why.

So tell me,
what's right about this life
I have lived?
Surely, you know there's beauty
in the gentlest of things,
and that wonder will raise ears
every now and then.

Listen,
when I sing you
sweet lullabies.

For there's a little truth
in my every word.
There's a tear track
for my every sad thought.
There's a breaking smile
from my every joyful belief.

So answer me
with the two most righteous words,
should I ask:
"When you come by,
do you pick up
something you've left behind?"

Because if you say "yes",
then I'll learn to leave behind.
Yet if you say "no",
then I'll accept that your faith is true.

Because to me,
you will always be
the most beautiful girl in the world.
And should you see your beauty in me,
I'd be the happiest man alive.

So look down now
with pride
as I confess another little truth.

All I know has been
proven wrong by you.

Yet when your losers become keepers,
emotional figures don't lie.
For your happiness only seems to make liars figure
when you tell me a little truth.

The 45th Birthday Poem

In the words of the saints:

Old, new
Moses, Jesus
judgment, mercy.

I needed the genes and so did she.

By faith, life becomes a glass ladder to salvation's sky.
By doubt, love becomes a struggle to combine the *Holy Trinity*.

Piecing together the torn paper
of what would be my 45th birthday poem,
all at once I grow completely calm as she blesses the room.

And though she and I become confused,
I remember that indignation's conception is a glass ladder to the sky;
I remember that the *Holy Trinity* is the human condition to combine.

Because Jesus said:
"*He who has no sin, may he cast the first stone.*"
Because Moses said:
"The spirit is the foundation of the heart, not the soul."

Here I had been, trying to save myself with a past,
the future that got forgotten as her existence touched mine
with a love that replaced trust in myself with life's *'everybody else'*.

In the words of the poets:

Love, lust
paranoia, perversion
fear, hope.

I needed a scene and so did she.

Yet through acceptance, she existed in me and I in her.
Through change, there was an absence that called for progress.

And though paranoia made repression into perversion,
I found love in the presence of lust that forsakes the cross;
I found hope in the fear that pursued the reality of loss.

Because Jesus said:
"Plant righteous seeds and a garden will grow."
Because Thomas said:
"No doubt can blind an ambitious faith."

Yet on this birthday, I had forsaken doubt for faith's cross.
With this generation, I had made new what the past had lost.

We each have moments and this was one of them.
"You got a haircut!" I stutter. This was good news, after all.
News richer, more tangible than a spending man's wallet.

"Can you feel it?" she beams.
The womb of happiness is God's force of habit.
"Smarter than a wallet," I attempt to please.
"Your wallet," she says.

Because Jesus said:
"Time can heal all wounds."
Because Judas said:
"Remove time and all is possible."

"I could have waited longer," I boast as she laughs at me.
Dishonest pleasure is a poor excuse for unheeding's humor.
Only this time was different. Now she carried a generation.

I needed to bleed and so did she.

Keeping your Girl Clutch High

There's nothing like a girl clutch high
to make the diamonds sparkle inside her
eyes of smiles and 'why's'.
I know she can't tell me otherwise.
There's nothing like a long white dress
and a flower in her hair on the day she
goes with me down the stairs...
the day she tells me how much she cares.
I know there's another place somewhere... out there.
There's something to be said about the little girls who
smile up at men and tell them their secrets
as if they understood them.
I know the old know many things... like this and there.
But I can't tell her this right now... because she's not here,
and all I understand is the rain that comes down
in the band-playing sun.
The music starts harder, now that she's not here to
stand alone with me.
I know she can't hear me now... but I hear her
every time she's gone.
So I push the clutch down... and all the others
laugh and say how much she is to me. But there isn't a single other
one I'd
miss more than she.
I love her because she understands this
and what it means to leave.
There's nothing like a girl clutch high
to send you smiling inside another's eyes, to
tell them why you're saying good-bye, and why
she says: "No more... no more good-byes."
I like her hair when it blows in my dreams I've forgotten.
I like the way the others tell me the wind is for her like the sky is
for me.

But I don't understand anything when she
leaves. All I feel is the rest of heat and all the motion, cold,
when she tells me that she understands me better than she.
And all I know is how foolish I am for having
spent most of my life gathering
telephone messages in my dreams and
putting puzzles together in my schemes.
She is the one I speak to now, because she is in me.
And I know that the clutch must go on high
if she is not to leave.
And I want to turn her head back inside of me
and tell her why she must not leave.
Because, for me, there's nothing like a woman who understands she
must be strong and of a good courage.
And all the rest of them will understand, when she and I have
gone out to that special someplace... out there.
They'll write down a memoir and tell the children who look up at men
how far it is to go to that girl clutch high.

Reiki's Pink Vegas Levitation

Only the energy in her hands can keep me company
when she proceeds to press her lotioned palms firmly
down the center, then butterfly out across my bare chest—
the reiki heat that releases melatonin like curves create intelligence.

Fingers are our favorite weapon. Hands can lock and load experience.
Massage is the goal, as I heave up and down out of pleasure's control.
I return the gesture by brushing back her strands of hair that cover
her inverted mouth as she kisses mine as tight as brand new shoes.

In dreams, I catch her karma's inner child, floating, as our bubbles join,
place my serious wand into her magic skin until my size weighs her down.
She prepares her eyes for impact. Reborn, I pop out of her womb— intact.
The Sin of tiptoe rules envelops memory as I drip from the vee of her hips.

As long as we can bet on each other's getting of *'I do'*,
we'll start over when premature plays beg for posthumous ends.
Only after the curves of allure can enlighten no more,
will we cease to call on kindred spirits to calm the waters of pretend.

The effects of lust cause us to afford the gifts of the Lord,
until energy wanes from the waxing of procrastination's latitudes.
Adorned with the pheromone armor of charm's unborn,
we kiss each other's bliss as arms feed our naked gratitudes.

Because after the sun goes down, only reiki hands can keep us company,
interrupt rhythm's beat with the faking of innocence that makes heat abrupt—

172

the ripple of skin that makes fickle hands swim against the deviance of jazz,
to levitate experienced newly-weds across the threshold of pink Vegas dives.

Rubbing my blue-framed eyes, I stand to make a high-wire trip to the bathroom.
Balling my wet hands, I punch showered arms through my last untraveled shirt.
My hair meshes with her pillow's bowl of flesh while I leave her dreaming there.
What happens will stay, they say. She smiles as the door cuts through the air.

My rich genes have stopped consuming these unhanded-down slots,
the obsession with loss that fails to master abundance's timely game.
I've come to date neon ghosts of gold streets with car-covered frost—
parked debts in netted yards of signed skies and butter-climbed faith.

Wiping the Face of Venus

I forget not to think until she sleeps.
I care to know how much she can bear.
I learn by remembering when she weeps.

Nothing is present without procrastinating.
Procreation obligates with justification's scars.
Arrogance hurts ambition for alienation to attract healing.

I think of missing pleasures she has hidden deep.
I hear her crying when her thoughts are lain bare.
I forget not to think until she sleeps.

Abuse excludes and use includes hating.
Dreams cage lost souls within golden bars.
Nothing is present without procrastinating.

Sweat weakens her like tears in speech.
Sorrow's game is always played by two.
I learn by remembering when she weeps.

Loving sweats hunger with the moans of mating.
Lust angers men into doing regretful acts.
Arrogance hurts ambition for alienation to attract healing.

Her cave wells up whenever she senses my desire.
Her curves cut blues like a diamond woos.
I forget not to think until she sleeps.

Giving seeks guilt until danger is found.
Righteousness pays dues with population's tax.
Nothing is present without procrastinating.

Then I string her with foam like the moon waves a beach.
We make out until I've taken all she has to share.
Afterwards, I learn by remembering when she weeps.

Hope wipes the face of hurt when we stop aching.
Fear remembers desire's ever-fleeting stars.
Together, arrogance hurts ambition for alienation to attract healing.
Dirty laundry keeps lying clean. To wife is to grace a street.
Sin comes from knowing. Marriage is caring's prayer.
I forget not to think until she sleeps.
I learn by remembering when she weeps.

Good deeds save punishment. Forgiving blesses betraying.
Charity compromises when Venus becomes Mars.
What is ambitious is arrogant. Procrastination attracts by alienating.

Immaculate Exposure

34th birthday over.
I guess not everyone can outlive Christ.
43rd birthday yet to come.
My address is Ostend, Belgium.
For when I was 12,
I sought to be perfect like *'Fire and Rain'* by Taylor.
Then when I was 21,
I imagined how Marvin shrove without saltpeter.
Still, I learned his palindrome pressure
between savvy yin and naïve yang.
Still, I learned his energy's release
that kept him pushing the envelope with his music.
So if I should marry,
let it be with one older, another younger.
If I must divorce them both,
let my side of the story go platinum.
Only when I turn 81,
may I come back like Henry Fonda to 18.
Only when I'm on the *Grammy's*,
may I have enough humility to kiss the award.
Just don't forget to keep a room for me *On Golden Pond*
when America calls on me to perform.
Just don't forget that fame is my Achilles' heel
when I'm too sold-out to postpone the tour.
For here I am in D.C., struggling to see at 15
the grand finale through binoculars,
trying to join a silhouette of fans on their feet—
an act that has my step-father pressed to leave.
Here I am lip-synching with the crowd
the delicate phrasing of Marvin's new motif,
now intermission lines of influence rasped out,
until the audience's climax of foreplay's bared underwear
makes the acne girls in the good seats go crazy

and the smiling spouses sway their longevity faith—
when I listened for immaculate exposure
to parallel my free association
with the song keyboard player Odell Brown
worked on when Marvin had nothing
but Freddy Cousaert's kidnapped optimism over boob tube plaster
regulations.
There I was leaving your original sin,
that angled manipulation of a wireless mic.
There I was exiting the arena of your carpe diem,
not realizing that this magic would never come again.
For passion is chosen during puberty's innocence,
the reason all the children wish to understand
why playing your music keeps me nervously pacing,
building up a catharsis that only seems to perpetuate
my need to strain with arms raised and eyes closed—
the deification of Marvin's new red silk, pajama aesthetics.
Maybe idolatry is like waiting in the wings
for your favorite star to preach his familiar farewell pitch,
promote that new album with only one hit song.
For Taylor only sang covers to gain popularity.
For Marvin only stripped to mirror Prince's hype.
Yet female alienation can take the social gambler out of a man,
attend wounds with proud acquiescence, save love from fear.

Jogging in Place

As in the *Romans 7 Rule,*
I'm divided by the spirit and the flesh,
like a god torn between Sophia and Jesus.
Yet, somehow, if I remain in between,
you'll come back to stay with me
here in room E809.
So I jog in place until my key opens the door.

Canceling out both extremes,
like the bed that has become our resting place,
we become slaves to its past sins
as our bodies grace its horizontal elevation.

Once my evil fought was my evil sought.
Now I seek your good to fight against evil.
Because salvation and temptation may coexist,
yet possession is transient.
In finding its dependence,
we are moved by good's freedom
and all that it has to offer.
Does not love exult and lust degrade?
Is not salvation an absolute reality
that lust chooses to imitate?
Is not temptation possessed at its peak
between dusk and dawn?

Here at midday we lie on a bed without sheets
as cares drift around us.
I sit at your feet where guilt had made me celibate,
after deciding to take down the girl poster
that would float desire above my head.

Where is that old baseball, dear friend?
Tell me of the next year on 207 Bay State Road,
(yes, a brownstone!),
where I would leave you behind a note and graduate.

From this window, let me see the *Citgo* sign
that transforms every night electronically
while the Kenmore Square traffic comes and goes
in the rain like breaking waves.

Let me look at myself in the mirror I once cried in
as I listened to *'Touch Me in the Morning'*,
as I realized that a female acquaintance had less to say.

Let me learn to change my feelings once again,
propped upon the back of that wooden chair,
accept from you another faithful poem,
unlike the sexually-languished all-night entropies
only my professors could see through.

How can I forget the space beneath that bed-spring,
where my Sony boom-box would usually be stored,
where I could honor the ascetic notion
that the absence of music could make me grow closer
to the higher learning this university could bring.

I wipe the dust from the stained shelf above your head
where my *Mother Church Bible* had been,
where I would move its bookmark from the page
in Ecclesiastes that proclaimed: *"All is vanity."*

At my old dormitory desk,
I write for you a poem I could never write then,
when Edie Brickell's *'Circle'*
and Womack & Womack's *'Teardrops'*
played in the background,
when my father told me over the phone

that he was 'getting a divorce',
when inhibition gave me new reasons to fast again.

"Relax!" my fatherless roommate would demand,
as I would wander like a troubadour
through my address book for a number
I could reluctantly call for familial support.

Now married to your psyche,
I thank someone for having answered my prayer,
remember how he had used
my *Super 8* silent movie camera on me
while I lip-synched '*She Drives Me Crazy*'.
Until, without a trace of my omens, you moan,
tell me about being glad I shared your hot fudge sundae
from the cafeteria downstairs.
Your cross-examination helps me to make my decision.
"I think I'll take a shower," I say with pride.

That's how everything had changed,
how forever replaced past connections by a future
which our feelings wished would remain.
"I think this room is good... after all,"
you smile, assist me as I peal my wet new shirt off my back.

In E809, I write for you this poem,
cross bare floors to a public bathroom
for the hot and cold mixing of reunion plans,
after suits split like a playing card deck
shuffled until rest becomes motion, chaos order.

Dancing Hippocratic Hype

I often watch leaves blur life beneath the soiled feet
that mash spoiled fruit left for the downpour of rain,
returning them to the dust you and I have reaped,
like leaf scores blossom sleep into leap day expectancies.

For deception moves over when winters fall to earthly bodies,
as soul springs into what cardiac summers do to pulses slowed,
when emotions unlock smiles like church greeting pamphlets.
Receptiveness meets burdens as the bell tolls its perfect relativities.

I wasn't the one Rosa liked though you made me want
her guilty eyes and your restless desire to flaunt.
I slipped into class after our alternate lunch-break romp
when never and forever dance Hippocratic hype.

I took to girls with the buckteeth and stares,
the ones no one looked at just because they cared.
One Valentine's Day, a card's quarter fell through the air
as never and forever danced Hippocratic hype.

There is an oath of unequal rights opted-out for democracy,
of the glories of people married to states like prearranged furniture.
I call it the weather of capitalism, unpredictable traffic management.
We all animate godly doubts when burning bushes obliterate labored
funds.

Can you see how progress uproots unfinished work like sowing seeds
cups lazy hands into frozen petals of bitter cold's morning dew,
reverses misfortunes into needs, blurs meandering chalk finish lines,
answers calls with neutrino breezes, warms us within celestial
wombs?

I got into the good of the high school I couldn't take,
took a bus home alone as poems suffered the grade.
Only the theatre arts teacher could tell me what was at stake
when never and forever dance Hippocratic hype.

I attended a Carolina college, colored my words to the sky,
fought my fundamental self with half the will of rye,
dared to read a book because the minister could cry
as never and forever danced Hippocratic hype.
Some tell of careless children whose tempers camp-out alone,
trespass plastic plateau reservations of Californian wealth,
the glamorous greed that needs no TV introduction.
America triages success because buried dreams live longer deaths
than fame.

We accept that which never changes, hold onto things bruised and
forsaken.
These days are like luring bait: the fish groan what their empty
stomachs ate.
Yet rebirths replace dead of night impatience with substitution's
survival pests,
gather grief like the *extra's* of experience. The work of love is never
done.

I communicated in Boston, old enough to drink,
prayed for the letters quickly scribbled with ink—
walked right on by as she took time to think
when never and forever dance Hippocratic hype.

I grew up too fast for our failed marriage to earn
the beauty of youth, a second shot at the sermon,
tattooed a Puerto Rican with rights she returned
as never and forever danced Hippocratic hype.

Some tell of emergency weekend hangars for solar-powered ultralight jets,
the bullets of faith that squall for thrills like alienated momma boys,
intercept bougainvillea fires like flies dismissed from trash can
church sin.
Damp vessels ride storms along long and winding air until calm
smashes ashore.

All we have are its plastic attitudes, the limits of its euphemistic
inflexibility.
Tell me *for real* if you have ever seen a leap day score become
complete
or a missed traffic light taken for granted only flash from yellow to
green?
Doubt not faces when they believe you're everything. They want to
be seen.

I busted my buttons when my old neighbor told me,
he got the religion of Southern hospitality,
applied my degree of pity and envy psychology
when never and forever dance Hippocratic hype.

I've since married gowns that hover sinks of soapy silverware,
after tucking sleepy ones under clouds of pillow-talk affairs—
tarried the magic that stings paws like honey-tricked bears
as never and forever danced Hippocratic hype.

Elimination Submission

I miss you here; I find you there:
I fall in love with you everywhere.

Spoiling ourselves creates greed.
Neglecting others creates loneliness.
Spoiling others creates selfishness.
Neglecting ourselves creates trust.

They say that beauty touches us in different ways.
I shake alone in the dead of night thinking about you.
How long will it not be before the thawing of your heart
can melt greed's abuses with the paths of trust's uses?

There was once a weakness in me and you.
Now there is but a healing strength in between.
There was once a restlessness of laughter
that lifted our prayers from bended knees.
Now we farm the beach beneath our wet feet
with the footprints that fade like mirrored hearts.

You kiss me here; you lose me there:
we call on each other's beliefs everywhere.

I suppose the time has come
for you to grow beside my pride.
I guess there are only younger loves
to mirror the ones we've planted inside.

I cannot prove that my loyalty is saltier
than the warm tears that roll down cold cheeks,
only that ice crystallizes pine trees with winter's weight
when I wake to dawn like a bear at the end of hibernation.

So give me your naked hand like old friends do.
Blush a bit before you bring yourself to accept
affection's greatest gift and utter a childish yes.
I may not promise that I'll submit to the process of elimination,
only that I want to laugh when my expressions please
and need to cry when you hurt me with unanswered whys.
I miss your kiss here; you find me lost there:
we call for lovers to fall in love everywhere.

I suppose there is no greater love
that keeps us planted by one another's side.
I guess in as many ways I prayed for God above
to make mutual feelings the reason we're alive.

Pleasure is entropic, like the quickening flames
that ravish the heart by the gusts of the soul's winds.
Pain is transient, like the sluggish floating of black clouds
that splatter our earth's saturated soil with the mind's rains.
Love perpetuates like an undisposed proposition.
It consummates by the process of elimination's submission.
We fall in love to gather the fragments of our puzzled drift,
until warm tears roll down cold cheeks and all the pieces fit.

Wabi Sabi Tsunami

You'd be gazing out your window about now;
thinking about the day ahead of the snow's cold.
I'd be in the shower getting ready to warm my car;
waiting for winds to free leaves from rain's wet hold.

Leaf peepers keep gathering around here
every year
since you left them near:
to witness the birth of dying colors.

Whenever I look in the mirror,
I see their fascination with color in your eyes:
not the misty gleam I once believed in,
but the one you only shared with this sky.

I've remained here like a sunset,
alone, the gradual evolution of objectivity
that entombs lies of deliberate, genetic desperation
within nature's Russian doll of truth's entropic tsunami,
until exodus unsheathes genesis like capsized laughter.

We have driven around these parts
many times before we could seem fit
for our every glance we'd cast toward each other,
only to learn that they were for the crowd's benefit.

Early each morning, the sea gulls of Schoodic sit
along the endless granite,
transfixed by the distant buoys of lobster traps,
as if waiting for love's calming consummation to return.

They help me to gather all that hasn't come true:
the idle inspiration that makes my dreams a little higher,
like the strange girls who feed the fire of desire's muse
by selling me the right to read the wrongs of their smiles.

At high tide,
I watch waves catapult to the heavens—
masters of the surf
lust's profusion still captures in my lap
like a black cat,
until wabi sabi has served extinct expectations.

Unforsaken

Let's unwind,
and teach each other your true love rhymes.
Count the time.

Your story
is the kind that steals all the glory.
I worry.

There's a joy
in the women who loved me so coy.
I'm your toy.

We can laugh
'cause I know that you want me to have.
I'm so glad.

I could not
tell the world that I would tie the knot:
if you're bought.

Should I stray
when our dreams seem an ocean away,
I will pray.

Feeling blue,
I show the world how my love is true...
when with you.

If too low,
I may cry but I'll know that you know.
Let me know.

Tears of trust
fall like rain from the skies up above,
like His love.

So just stay
but a while before you go away.
What you say?

Until you
retire from the work men put you through,
I'll be true.

With your faith,
I will follow and not disobey
serenades.

Love remains
when we learn how to let it remain
every day.

Like a dove,
fly back proud to all the ones who must
forsake love.

Bohemian Bought Equality

I am, therefore she must be—
the one I love more than He.
She is the rainbow, therefore I must go
to the family that marries *'please stay'* with *'leave me'*.

The time is always short, the children born always near.
Her sanctified womb she obeys like her chastity birthday.
This midnight, she's strong. I suffer for her sore morning.
Life. Love. Work. These three are judgment's *Holy Trinity*.

We accept pain to accept pleasure, show each other mercy.
I am the change coming that makes fathers ill-prepared and young.
To survive, we learn to seesaw between surrender and empathy.
To change is to accept rebirth— relinquished bohemian-bought
equality.

Her water broke late that evening. He had stayed up all night praying.
She called the ambulance herself, waited by the lobby, incontinent,
alone.
I am the son of a charity that betrays church, government, scientific
communities.
What is a woman, if not another's servant? All men struggle with
strange hospitality.

It is our animal nature to judge the poor, kiss and tell the lies of
corrupt authorities.
Scripture is sociological. I give because I have taken, gained because
I have lost.
I sometimes hear her siren spinning wild inside. It saves like butter
sells bleached bread.
See me exiting Wheaton Plaza as a *'Darkman'* whispers his gospel
of life's library ledge.

Where there is snow, there is clay. Where eyes heavy, dopamine deepens with sleep.

I am not home yet closed. My sacrifice is but good business, my servants are my King.

I must learn to keep her safe, if I am to warrant her sofa privacy, solicit her secret business.

I feel the people rest. Come share this pink sky with me. Life is bitter cold, shocking, sweet.

Love is Always Fair

I was waiting. Didn't know the reason.
I just felt that it was the season to stay alive with you.
Because I was never so much in love
until I saw my world next to you.

And darling, I don't know if I can reach you.
Still, I'm gonna try to teach you the love that I once knew.

You can tell by the simple nail file
that keeps my hair from blowing wild,
I'm never afraid the phone is tapped
and love is always fair.

Love is like breathing. Love is what you swallow
when you follow someone through the darkness,
until you hear the chirps by the light of day-birds singing.

Let me say, there's nothing like a wedding ring.
How can I talk about children while I'm still
just a fellow hanging by your string?

Because there's a little joy in everything you desire.
There's lots of sorrow in the things that you don't really need.
And although life is rarely fair, love always is
when you let yourself be led by someone.

You can tell by the penny count that jar the banks,
that the golden egg is broken each day by empty truck tanks.
I'm never home when my mail is locked and addressed
and love is always fair.

Ain't it sweet to have known life nearly gone and then complete?
Ain't it wonderful to have been given such grand notions,
only to be taken by a beauty so young and petite?

I must be borrowing something precious for me to tarry.
There's lots of reasons for me to marry the past to the tomorrow
that I've learned to borrow with the present of you.

All my days... I was counting them like yesterdays.
I was praying like they would never stay...
because I was simply much too afraid.

You can't tell by my sad smile, yet my style breaks like the Nile—
where lightning zaps the Red Sea and saps gravity from thunder
miles.
My prophesies are never exact when you remind me how promises
stack
and love is always fair.

Let's plea-bargain, talk of money gardens
that attach proteins to antibody-sick, God healing,
couple jouncing legs with facial dancing,
just because reloaded gift cards bleed lines.

Let's unboard merchandise of foreign-price demand,
saturate politics with *Marvel* on a billion-dollar scale,
until the satellites call our Copyright history up for sale by frequency—
the dreams we've lost to other folks spinning on strange, tender
hands.

You can't tell which traffic signal will let your motor not blink
and wrap your ring finger with pokadot *pellieres*, scurry forest
fresh air.
And which love is always fair you may think ain't.
Yet love is always fair.

Because I've dated honeymoon-time,
ordered refills over beer and wine—
just remember that broken lives love working minds.
And which soul gets the baby and which goes to heaven
cannot be smitten from the danger and the beauty written
on the hearts that know how love is always fair.

Quixote's Witness

Are you still running from dreams that won't come true?
Can you still see my face there— half-lit by sunlight,
as they call the event only my father can make you race?

Had I knew that there was a science for every mind...
a glance at your size to remove the concept of time,
I would have let you know.
Had I knew that there was a history to every line...
a psychology for the reasons only some of us rhyme,
I would have let you know.

"Just give it your best shot," I say, as the other runners rustle
their spiked sneakers into motion's ever-smoking cinders.
For after you hear the crack of the referee's adrenal gun,
I will set your pace as you loom around the track eight times:
the only difference being an incremental ruffle in your hair.

For there are moments in between the laps of Don Quixote
that cut a canyon of dreams reality cannot erase—
leave a river of illusions to erode rest like wrinkles tear upon a face.

If I could do it all over again, I wouldn't have called after you hung up...
I wouldn't have challenged the strategies that made us chess friends.
Because had I knew that you were the one who confuses
and refuses to let the other soul witness...
had I knew that our promises kept empty shadows walking alone,
I would have let you know.

Side by side, you and my father thrash masochistically,
as pistons pierce gravel down the straight-away.
Arms paddling your rib-cage... you pick up speed, catch the wind.
Can I ever forgive you for charging into my father's windmill—
trying to prove that you were a better Sancho Panza?

Because ever since you married, everything's gone wrong it seems...
like a fire in my own backyard— there to remind me of how
intolerance blurs.

Because had I knew that anger would make me neither sacred nor
profane...
had I knew that gaining hunger would leave me neither honest nor
blamed,
I would have let you know.

For it is only jealousy cheering you on, as you lunge past me and the
finish line...
the solitary father who lifts your chin with such class as he and I
begin to cry.

Yet it is *my* father who helps you to feel the sin of betrayal that wins
the final turn...
the fissionable fusion of sweat that chooses passion over what
relationships split,
like the opposite sex of 'me' cannot prove love's lack of energetic
transience
nor the same sex of 'you' remove the deprivation of lust's REM-sleep
entropy.

Because had I knew that holding on is but a bent-knee activity, for
Thomas to see
how Judas kept his wineglass spent— I would have let know that we
were through.

The Way Lightning Spurs

I was looking out the window,
saw the wind blur everything so.
Never did I ever save you before,
the way that the lightning spurred.

Then I came, I saw my face
in the reflection of the blackened space.
I never thought that I would have to blur
the reason I left you, the way lightning stirs.

Where did I have my heart and soul?
Did you take it when you went and go
to the store, the places you know.
I never thought I would love you so.
But I saw the lightning... saw the lightning spur.

When you came back, I knew you would haul
all those things that you left in the hall.
I never saw, but I knew that you sawed
every tree and every lawn.

Where did you ask me to pick you up?
Did you tell me to load up my truck?
Now I know that I'll never stir
feelings left like the lightning spurred.

The lightning spurred, I knew you would hide...
knew that could never tell me why.
But I know that as long as you heard,
I will love you like the lightning spurs.
I will love you like the lightning spurs.

When did you go to my heart?
When did you tear it into the start
of a storm that sows my soul,
sows every lightning, spur and go
to the places where the lightning spurs.
Take me to the places the lightning spurs.

Boston Moon

He hates the sun because
she loves the moon.
Father of my pride;
mother of my desire:
makes perfect sense to me.
Behold, love is a fourth moon;
the phase that receives
from the spirit
what the flesh conceives.

Someone please tell me
what I need to know
when all that remains true
is the doubt that wanes
among earth's worded ruins
that surface this city
like a lifetime
of forgotten dreams
from the mind that dares
to return to the garden
knowing well that it's sin
that makes us see.

Behold, love is a third moon;
the phase that relieves
the body with all
that the soul can perceive.

Someone please tell her
that the only thing
that changes is the light
that shines from within
like the white

that swallows words
pounding through paper
like blood without flesh.

See, I love the word because
she hates the word.
Fighter of my faith;
lover of my trust:
makes perfect sense to me.
Behold, love is a second moon;
the phase that grows
with all our laughter,
with all our tears.

Only notice how it waxes
when we forget to look
upon its beckoning face.
Learner of my life;
master of my death:
makes perfect sense to me.
Behold, love is a first moon;
the phase we all go through.
Keep it new when he comes for you.
Find it full when it's me you seek.

Sudden Smile Relief

(for Shanika)

When I was found by her,
I thought the wedding was over
beneath the hot air lanterns of prayer.
Between us, the bay rippled like her hands
waved gestures into *'nowhere's'*.

People say that the good
give to get and the bad
take to leave, that its paradox
may clear my conscience.
People say that competition
is only for the wrong,
compromise for the right.
And people request prayers
from the congregation
that I might find someone
who can teach me how
in trusting we need love,
that it's greed that wants war.

For the way I left her
kept me consumed, at a loss to say
how one survives acts of midnight's insatiable requests.
She didn't seem to care if I walked alone somewhere.

It didn't even matter
that some people hugged me
when I was too stubborn
to learn from the gall
that overshadowed me
or too lazy to think

on their wavelengths,
until I learned to walk the tightrope
that trust provides between greed and grace.

Because distance is like
a genesis of being:
it'll give you guts
connecting with the stars
before they can contract
and make you nuts
to imagine what lies
beyond their expanding.

Only try not to confuse
the implications of a runaway
universe with religion's truths
as they cross your mind.
Only don't waste the sun's fuel
on the dreams that make you
light enough to long for heaven
when the world's weight
is gravitating towards you.

You see, the way I left her,
I've come to accept her need to supply
the comfort that left my waiting to honor her demands.
She has come to see me in a new light I hear everywhere.

For angels only sleep
with those who believe
that they can still be saved.
And the devil only works
through those who cannot say
the poetry in their hearts,
those who'd rather ask how

God could give birth to sin
and then demand praise
than to recognize the rainbow
that guides our rainy days
through the silhouette I've come to see
behind the fragrance of fire
that joins our hands like stems from a flowered vase,
spreads interests like compatibility's big bang revelation.

Still, the way I left her,
the winter heat keeps me sweating thorny petals
of neglected statements of our undecided affairs.
Apart from her, I've left some feelings unanswered,
questioned most of my thoughts,
even woken myself from my wildest dreams.

It seems that proximity
leads us to believe
that there is truth in inequity
and who am I to doubt it?
It seems that we lose control
when everyone mocks us
for choosing to share
the insecurity that is not without pride
and who are they to deny our vanity?

And so I stand up alone
to take in the crowd
for my fifteen minutes of fate
as they try to imagine
being in our shoes.
I look them each in the eye
and relish the luck
that would not be mine
were it the other way

and pray that our faith can give birth
to their own navel contemplation
and who are they to refuse?
See how it does them no good
to complain about our having learned
to live the life they envy so.

Perhaps a lover is *not* destined
to be as lonely as a cloud,
the bliss of solitude
I have desired for myself for so long
and who am I to not need,
to not want more?
For fate seems to keep me
wandering the rusted bars
of life's precarious jungle gym
that, though often ending
where you once began,
fails to lead you where you wish to be,
unlike love's crystal stair.
So I carefully balance
with each and every step
through the dangers that keep me
on my feet as I try to imagine
meeting you on the other side
of the pride that moves this world
around the promises that make up
the created risks of success
no woman dares not let her man test
out of fear of losing the hope
that makes it easier for them to fall in love.

For my hunger gives and my anger takes
the eat and sleep of her sudden smile's relief,
the prescription that circulates blood

like a critical sacrament,
moves us closer to the axis of becoming whole,
until I learn to pay as much attention
to her high heels as to her working shoes,
attempt to heap conviction
with stubborn sleep's weeping deep,
turn the flesh into the consensual obligations
of the spirit's perpetual beliefs.

Not until now does she jinx every pool shark's best shot
off the banks of even the heaviest camouflaged stare
with that sudden smile relief I've come to please, the way I left her.

Attraction Loss Idiot Savant

I married someone who tells me how to think.
She says I know too much but have a deprived mind.

I carry her inside me like I'm a wordless vessel.
I say she's thicker than water and that I use her like ink.

For when we go out, we enjoy each other's company.
And when we get home, we're as gentle as pets.

Because we've got the vibe it takes to stay together.
Because we've learned how to live beyond past reservations.

If I inevitably return to the blank page full of thoughts,
still she waits to read what results from born-again oblivions.

So call me nuts, yet I'm determined to flatter her ways.
Because when I imitate them, she reasons with me by touch.

And when I think the way she wants me to,
I relish the grand illusions I get from a deprived mind.

Because when I get lost, I suffer like an artist
just to learn from her attraction loss like an idiot savant.

Because should I neglect myself, she'd only laugh like a child
and beg for me to give her a spanking to spoil her innocence.

Should someone look her over as we pass them by,
she'd just hug me from behind and cry: "Come on, babe!"

Still I get excited by her restless boredom, oh my!
She's more than one man can work and I ain't playin'.

For my girl suffers from attraction loss to keep me satisfied.
Because sexual sobriety connects the freak with foolish propriety.

And when her two qualities get feedback from boundless honesty:
part of me gets lost in the shuffle; part of me goes blind.

Because attraction has a way of tempering patience with luck,
like when she gives me another chance to ignore what lacks.

Because loss has a way of making peace with wrong omissions,
like when I complain until I commit to the intelligence that tasks.

Perhaps one can never be faithful enough when romancing
the only woman who can make *his* grass the most green.

Perhaps men need to learn how to take advice from women
when confronted with a blank page and in need of ink.

You see, I accept the changes she puts me through.
For when I get *too* swank: she straightens my back; bends my knees.

And even if I must call her the moments I travel so far she cannot
stay:
still she fades time; sounds relief; jades feelings; bounds belief.

She says I know too much but have a deprived mind.
I married someone who tells me how to think.

Where Lilies Sweep

Perhaps lovers know it the best.
For all the Gentiles clothe it to make it their law.
Because whenever they deviate or conform,
they try to change one another by yang's lust
or long to give more effort by yin's love...
while we simply stay in our element;
while we can choose to change like the wind.
And if you're able to roam with me
among the lilies of the *Gospel of Matthew*,
graze its fields until your joy overflows.
Should I lose every ounce of my courage
when you learn what to do,
accept my trust as open as my heart's view.
For gravity doesn't matter
when lilies move
by the wind that causes hearts to grow.
I don't know how long it will last for you.
I only know how easy
the tug comes and goes for me.
What I can tell you is this:
your happiness will always shine for me
like righteousness floats among the hills of Matthew.
For side by side,
we learn from the lilies of the field
that neither toil nor spin...
until we have no cares,
save the feelings we want to share
and the joys we hope the future will bring.

Until... down some avenue, we waltz again;
thinking of nothing but such dreams so true.
For walking beside you, I see how I had nothing
while girls played me for their boyfriend's loyalties

only so that *you* could become the woman of my dreams.
I think I'd be crazy to believe I could be with anyone else.

Suddenly, we see the light turn green,
and rush before the approaching traffic can quicken.
Love's thrill is all we need to know now,
when needing to seize the moment
makes our free souls too brave to behave.
Because what's on the other side we leave behind.
For life has made our charms evolve
from the days before they led us to today.

So lazy your running as we come to a halt.
Allow their interest to turn you the same way as me,
and watch the light change from green to red again
as idle passengers observe from half-open windows.
For looking at each other,
we can pick up from conversations that were never left off,
chatter until our words skip from beat to beat,
let our eyes meet exactly the way we hoped they'd meet.
Jesus instructed all twelve of his disciples,
saying: "Go nowhere among the Gentiles."
I say, find your love where the lilies sweep.

Picnic Posterity

In between the twists and turns,
we learn to give our trust
to every heart that wishes to be there
for us.
All around the corners and crevices,
we live to take it all
for each moment to live eternally
for them.
We are among the many,
among the few,
who bump into the destinies we wish each other
to see.
So greet them with the words I say...
before food makes their plates heavy
with beef.
Please their curiosity as you please me,
so that they might foresee the opportunity
that sits us both in lawn chairs until we balance rolls
between chips.
Because life is but a wink...
a breath we jump to take
while they rush through our lives blind to the fate
we create.
Life is at best a guess...
a thought we forget to erase,
as pickles wet fingers like gloves warm hands
with heat.
I don't know at what cost this comes to you,
or what this means
for us to make history out of the times
we've spent.
I cannot tell the friends from the future family
we may or may not be,

or how our hopes may later converge on two or more faces
drinking milk.
All I know is that whatever will be, will be...
after the crowd disperses and the sounds
become sweet.
Just let them hear the prayers we choose to keep,
for laughter to give us our second wind...
like leftovers
found in the grass and moments given to a joke's irony
to be both among the many and the few
belonging together.
Let these surroundings spread out to eternity
as we toss balls of opportunities to spread
our feet.
Keep talking through digestion until we all long to hear
the messages we plan to record for our mutual memory,
for posterity.
Learn to live the dreams we ask each other to sleep,
as our hearts find answers to the freedoms
chased by the moments we share
with reality.
Follow your intuition whenever it takes you
to picnics created out of the need to share
my company.

Biophilia's Homeostasis

Walking through Harvard Yard,
I catch the sights, the sounds.
Talking to a passer-by,
I fetch the local hot spot, the music store.
Looking for a street
that begins with the letter K,
I'm startled by the crackle
of a squirrel biting a nut.
Finding a busy corner,
I sniff cigarette smoke—
notice the straggler's ways.
Then I pick up the bus heading out of town:
closer to biophilia's homeostasis;
closer to my place of worship.
Rocking back and forth,
I pick up some old news— try not to listen
as a cell phone conversation begins:
remembering that 'being on time' is everything.
Until, with nothing but my soul to change,
I knock on your door and you are there...
as I accept your unleavened bread;
as I forget where I've been.
For there I know how kindness
means rewarding another in the name of grace.
There I can avoid the healing
that suffers in return for nature's cruelty.
Because we either live freely in our skin
or we suffer to live within another's.
And although I don't claim to know
the fruits of your life's searching,
truth brings me here each Sunday morning
so that I might grant you the right
to blame me for trying to preach

what you yourself have tried to know.
Because for me time keeps slowing down
as you welcome me home again with a smile...
while in your eyes I pretend not to see
how time has never spun so fast—
like the journey I take makes you wait,
longer and longer, the weekends I don't postpone
the hunger that gives less
and the anger that takes more:
the way biophilia sows hope
and homeostasis reaps fear.
So that, should my week end here,
I'll try not to think of the broken promises
that leave a woman without her means,
without the finger sandwiches and cups of tea,
and instead place my stock
in the trading of identities—
that always seems to open my eyes
to the offerings that succeed in returning
loss with wisdom or attraction with sneers...
as we saw through burden's warm chocolate
like floss and spread the thin blood of family
like coffee with aspirin.

The Labor Doctor

Good women are wise by nature,
ignorant of lies.
Buy the rich, bury the poor.
Good women sell souls through their eyes
like bullets through a prize.
See how their iris is a black hole
of praise that rises from children
like crows flock to stalks of corn?
Forget the plaid dresses, forget the fancy hats.
My women smile like they're "the one",
promise to erase the margin of error from loss.
How beautiful are good women,
wise in calculating the *'before's'* and *'after's'*
of players without game, those without pride.
Watch them take risks, fall for them.
I love good women because they don't cry.
Tell me, am I to doubt the labor doctors,
the machine gun girls
who rattle off luck like auctioneers,
every time good women hug good women,
pass on the lotto secrets to my success?
Good women, my women, stay the course,
wake dreamers to the truths only they know,
like details cultivate a crowd after accidents occur.
Other women only flatter certifiable practitioners,
pay for lasers, drugs, even surgery.
You only ask me to be patient
in return for making me yours,
trouble me with tough love when I'm lazy,
accept my gifts if they represent a holiday.
Still I complicate your venerable clearings,
blind to the results the sum of my parts has become.

Biological Universe

I need the energy found within God's biological universe.
Terror threats keep travel down while internet sales go up.
Wellness is America's religion, original sin the only constant.

Monsters mirror enemies within. Disease threatens the world.
Relationships become *the* science. Books preserve family histories.
Actors really do care more about our dreams than we do.

King Kong wins three Oscars. Godzilla stars, no Raymond Burr.
Wuthering Heights preserves pride's reality, *Star Wars* hate's myth.
Rocky Balboa returns to the ring at age 60.

Movies get less exciting every time you re-watch them.
I'm scratching my balding scalp for better circulation.

Love is a reality trip to the stars that shapes childhood identity.
Dark matter accelerates aging when we're not looking.
The three certainties in life are death, taxes, and gravity lines.

Mother earth gets hotter. Consumption thins the atmosphere.
Portable media delays echoes for boredom's synchronicity.
Cars are fueled by the sun and flatland corn.

I liked it better when love was just a fantasy trip.
Everything alien weighs more on the moon.
When parents turn *on* the lights, we decide to break the rules.

Politicians look the same holding up population's different flags.
Judas unveils a stellar riddle in a *National Geographic* magazine.
One generation later...

In our spaceship, we land on the moon.
You are pride. I am lust. They are hate.
In between the three of us: love.

They control us both: I get weaker, you stronger.
They give us blank instructions. We push all their buttons.
Authority returns innocence to two siblings in a spaceship to Eden.

The door opens. We bounce across the surface.
"Where's the flag?" you radio me before I regroup.
"Roger that," I signal back before we reenter the craft.

I need the energy found within God's biological universe.
Everything in dreams weighs more on the moon.
Our spaceship was, after all, just a poor blanket of hope.

Parental doubt heightens greed; pride lowers trust.
Siblings increase faith. Innocent hopes increase parental fears.
Marriage puts yin's pleasure and joy back into yang's pain and sorrow.

There are only two kinds of fantasies: one American, the other alien.
Children protect imagination because parents attempt to correct it.
Dreams escape reality's womb when God inhabits the biological
universe.

Glacial Climbing at Recess

My middle school friend leans against me at recess.
He says the low altitude and heat makes it that way.

The bullies stand, smiling, as cheerleaders line a brick wall.
We look ahead with the hope that they will help us to call their bluff.

We are glacial climbing at recess as we basketball play for trust.
They are friends of his. I am unwelcome at my old game lunch table.

Their future friends crawl a jungle gym as I ask, "What's the point?"
We yell, "Outstanding!" as they jump from its peak and crawl the grass.

The teachers grade papers at their window desks as we break a sweat.
They are more afraid of us than we are of their unannounced
pop-quizzes.

We are the adventurers, dream of inheriting their red ink, sports car suds.
I ask myself if they really care how long we have until the bell rings again.

Our kids will be the ones who ignore corrections, slam-dunk netted rims.
They will speak of overhead costs, generational divides, car wash twists.

A child either becomes a camouflaged lizard to wander zig-zag labyrinths
or a ray of B-line sunlight to borderline accents— an acute bowling
distraction.

Seek out the planets that hide in black holes. Remove inner-mountain
proof.
My cool friend shakes his fists at the hoop as I miss yet another blind shot.

Pondering Muhammadan Hieroglyphics

She is easy on these eyes. I watch them claim hard when non-issues
firework Armageddons.
She's on the verge of insane, tried irresistibility. I like it when she
sinks her needs into me.

Children skim mercy into our skin when lovers cream our solidarity
with perfect tea cup spoons.
Christ is idol talk to those who worship fame. The church knows the
family better than the name.

We turn a blind eye to judgment's loss when gain claims jealousy and
lies of blasphemous haste.
Compromises whenever your pride is craved. Explain your invisible
guilt with flames' desirability.

They are merging with us. Our reality pebbles their deep, covers
impartiality's autonomous feet
with REM-sleep, fathers transient entropy like a daughter gathers
equity together, piece by piece.

Art creates by love's second-guessing. Life pushes works in progress,
makes us wandering sheep—
tribes of mummified propaganda that soldier segregation to ponder
lost Muhammadan hieroglyphics.

The Lord's Air

I look in the mirror sometimes to see salvation,
only to behold the suffering from a past I had thought
was forgotten.

One boy's trash is another boy's tragedy.
I pull chosen hearts to forsake passion's pushed rhythms.

I look through the windshield at other times to see traffic
fall out of sync with the gravity that slicks headlights past
yellow belonging.

One girl's sacrifice is another girl's saddening.
I bury flying stints under work and dig phobias out of complexity.

We are only saved by timing the sacred perspective
that dwells within redemptive instants, harries the bearing of selfish
suffering,
internalizes resurrection.

One's tortured yesterdays is tomorrow's Magdalene triumphs.
I look to listen while asleep and wake to near antipodal existence.

Our passive head which art the gift shared by an active heart:
hallowed be Thy organs. Thy endorphin come, Thy poetry be done
by the hands that plow the sands of circulating lungs. Amen?

No, it's just Zen.

So give us this breath, its circular nirvana, and forgive us our oxygen
as we forgive their carbon dioxide. And lead us not by testosterone,
but deliver us with estrogen. Amen?

No, it's just Zen.

For Thine is the pull, the push, and the half-life falling of fear—
that with every second, we may come closer to the hope
of the annihilation of apprehension. Zen?

Yes, Zen.

Give to live. Take to make. Receive to believe.
For where one stretches, the other rests.
Where meaning lies. He lies. Amen?

Yes.

But if God is Zen, as fragile as air floating
above life's vessels of union,
if He is as possessive as a virgin guarding her bleeding heart:

then I say amen,
say it with the belief in this thirsty water bowl. Lap thoughts like a horse
fulfills life's repressed inhibitions. What goes in must come out.

Eastern non-religion bustles while we sleep, lighting revelatory REM-prayer.
Approach beauty as you would danger, the way dew levitates lotus tongues
suddenly unwrinkled.
Those who hate pain, love company and are spoiled by men and women alike.
Those who crave pleasure, neglect women and despise men—
deserving of all,
accepting nothing.

So listen to the honks that blast burdens outside the night mirror,
read the sheep answers that nod automatic traffic like shepherd
good-byes,
flock intersections.

O Zen of Zens, unbuckle faith's obligations with air's indulgent,
deadline mentality!
One priest's cold sweat is another priest's holy water at break of day.

P.O. Banks Carry Ego Lifts

I believe in the man who has a love, the journey between sin and God.
I believe in climbing's final signs, the reception waiting for us in another life.

I know the timing that prays with joy, when chaos comes after all to destroy.
I know the needs that ask not to receive, the doubts that run alone and afraid.

Yet happy strength carries ego away like a P.O. bank lifts grief from the grave.
Mountain becomes a ditch, rivers streams. You tame that I may brave your dreams.

Right-brain minds are but an unanswered phone, creative wines of blind alone.
The frozen land is but a fire to the world that salts the sushi of finger-lake fish.

When she came back, she gained a man, only to lose his snot-eyed son.
Overhead, jets womb sickness as Mary lids happiness with authority's day.

The Tassel

The student in me loves your West
as I embrace my East.
For now I see
yin and yang in one graduating:
if I am to push you like the sun;
if you are to pull me like the moon.

I do not stir up or awaken love
until it is ready.
After all, what matters
is how we allow life to share our claims.

When I radiate every ounce
of your beaming dignity,
like possession makes every man
teach his woman of its use,
let me accept your will's
hold over me,
as you gloriously ebb and flow
like high tide's crashing waves.

Watching from a distance
only hearts can bridge,
my poetic lens captures your every whim.

I felt an oxymoron stall in my brain
when it moved for me.
For it took the entire graduating class
to make me realize that right was left
and left was right.

What began as an annoyance
of my shifting tassel's slide
between the corners of my cap,
I inevitably took my moment
to make the crucial adjustment,
as my classmates did the same.

Now *you're* next in line,
as life makes you into one of its providers.
Because we graduate by consuming the truth
while listening for the moral to the story.

I hear parents' voices lifting hands,
as friends call out your name.

And should you seize me
along with your degree,
find joy in knowing that the reward
for every good deed is patient kindness.

All we need to accept now
is how close we really are,
as we get lost in something as sure
as a tassel that has moved
from sun to moon:
fixed like our working days;
free like our dependent nights.

So long as there are
angry mornings and hungry evenings,
our prayers will dare us
like blue skies,
just as eloquence from eve's toss
will surround us,
like rings around new moons.

I do not stir up or awaken love
until it is ready.
After all, what matters
is how we allow life to share our claims.

Yet when we come to graduate,
we all must learn of heaven and earth's
exchange between the tension ebb
of creative cold
and pressured flow of clinging's
warm release:
to shadow the heart like rain does sun;
to brighten the mind like moon does night.

Poison Pill

(for Maria Bartiromo)

I've been looking...
looking for a reason
you've remained beautiful
for so long.
Sure, P.R. may have dwarfed my sincerity.
Perhaps hams like myself
eventually swallow their own poison pill—
become too fascinated by publicity.
Yet I've been looking...
looking for the season
you'll beat down the competition
with your generous smile.
For we only kick up our own dust
when the numbers go on vacation.
We only hold onto our own wallets
when grandmothers plan for the future
of their unknown misfortunes.

Yes, I've been looking...
looking like Little Richard
for the elusive credit that plays.
Looking for a reason
you've remained lonely
for so long.

I don't know how you cried...
cried for the lovers who barely tried.
Don't know how you lied...
lied for their mothers
to read the *Wall Street Journal.*

Yet I know you've been looking...
looking for a reason
for that generous smile.
Know that there is a season
for brushing back hair
just before going 'on the air'—
within and without the TV we share.
Still, I'll be looking...
looking for the musical chair
anyone missing one would seek.
I'll be somewhere on vacation...
watching you if I may
say how wonderful
you've made me feel today
as I looked for a reason,
other than that cup of coffee,
looked for the right emotions to not stray...
looked for the proper poison pill
that could keep them real enough
for you to want to use that generous smile...
make me happy enough to stay.
Because long-term happiness is a weekend
of short-term reasons to stay lonely.
And I want you to remain beautiful
for so long.

I Laughed, I Cried

Because movies have a way of healing, I let go.
Because Hollywood prayer has a swaying motion.
And DVD bonus footage goes by so slow.

I love the plots that tell me what I already know.
We watch our favorite actor with such devotion.
Because movies have a way of healing, I let go.

Even special effects can make a picture show.
I guess money ain't what it used to be.
And DVD bonus footage goes by so slow.

Soon going to the cinema becomes appealing.
Even if your fingertips are buttered for a fee.
Because movies have a way of healing, I let go.

Sometimes I long to exit the theater in the dusky glow.
I'm the fanatic who buys the classic restored from erosion.
Nonetheless, DVD bonus footage goes by so slow.

Sentimental scenes take me to where memories flow.
At times I think I'm surrounded by a surreal ocean.
Because movies have a way of healing, I let go.
And DVD bonus footage goes by so slow.

The Nature of Things to Come

From gold to green, the naked trees bloom
as I sit this afternoon to witness
the turning of things left undone.
From mold to dew, the bald grass thickens
as I crush its tender blades beneath my feet
and remember the leaves I've forgotten to turn.
For from baby curls to drying gray,
I've combed my hair with the moist breeze
that always seems to catch me unawares
as I lift my face once again to the afternoon's glare.
From thin torso and thick limbs to its reverse,
I try my best to hasten up the hills
between porch and street
as I remember your grin like yesterday:
telling me to take in the freshly-bloomed trees,
take in the dandelions that bleach
the tall grass like random grief,
and, like the winter before,
know all too well the stubborn advantage
that covers it each year with snow
as we try to forget
the time we've wasted in between.
Knows too well that we may wake
another afternoon to witness
the nature of things left undone
rather than the sun that sometimes brings
the warmth that follows me back to bed until I see
the brittle turning over of a new leaf
you've waited your entire life it seems
to help me to believe in a life,
the nature of things yet to come,
that so rarely introduces me to sleep
and welcomes and comforts like another's
opening and closing of doors each spring.

Vulnerable Healing

(for Jessica)

There are sins I've thoroughly enjoyed with you.
Just say good-bye if you need to cry.
No time to say hellos after said good-byes.
There are unpredictable graces I've gone through.
Just say good-bye if you want to smile.
No time to play out joys after playing out sorrows.
These are the dimensions of faith.
These are the sacrifices of never.
Because pleasures refuse to lie.
And when we fight against the truth,
try not to push the pain deeper than lost pride.
Because there is a time for unsealing letters
to discover the bad news inside.
There is a time for locking doors
to keep safe from what the mystery hides.
There is a time for turning over new leafs
with the fall of yet another year.
There is a time for ironing out lust's kinks
while hate's iron still can sear.
And I've heard the birds in dried up trees.
I've opened blinds to where the shadows reside.
I've believed in angels without wings
and carried love like a cross.
I've watched my youth become the past
and vulture age sneak up on me like a train.
I've been trapped by culture dogma
only to be surprised by freedom one more time.
Still, there are times to carry loads of groceries
from the back of your car to the front door.
There are times to go to bed weary
from the passing of days that never seem to close.

There are times for sudden awareness
to become the gradual ambition of ears;
afraid that the sound of thunder will wake
the little ones still managing to stay asleep.
There are times for sweet confessions whispered
when bitter ones become too annoying to keep near.
Because consumer Gaia only happens once in a lifetime
and heaven is a manifestation of the regret trying to love us
into the hate that lies within the sands of subterranean skin.
So let there be a time to accept moods underneath motivations;
knowing how emotions are easier to respect than stout reason.
Because to make love, partners must accept one another's psyches,
occupy their potential growths— the sunlight that sinks treasures
like sea currents conceal fish movements, the shadow altitudes
that float wings of flight, the way time pressures inhibitions like
birds speak
vulnerable healing through telephone wires, spills sweat like habits
from a hose—
those outdated rabbits of a single vice, hopping in and out of greater
sin holes.

Docetic Attraction

There was a time
when I thought that attraction was a word
that you understood
in between the agony and the ecstasy
of my seeing you come and go.

Yet now I know
that Doceticism is one word
you won't let go of to become the scene
that never returns nor leaves.

I used to think
that relations meant sexual sacrifices,
like the give and take of compromise,
when the body hungers to share
what the mind angers to control.

Yet now I know
how our Docetic attraction does both...
those sacred sensations
that change like pain and pleasure
in the entropic physicality and the healing mentality
that have now become
the fragile web of ambient energy around you and me.

For to where you will go, I cannot lead.
Yet you may know now
that the roads that will be taken by you,
I have known like the rote directions only you could give,
should you later wish us to follow them together.

For where you come from, I will always long to be...
like a fool humbled to see
the stunning changes to your perfect form
that make lust seem better than what it ought to be.

Still, who you will turn to every now and then
in your time of need,
will always remain your business to keep.
Yet I know now how those pleasures can heal you,
just as desire's entropy has healed me...
after your every 'no'
let me surrender to the fear of another trance...
that makes love's victims hope to hear
one another talk within the wonder of reality's sleep.

Because who I confide in is only *our* business,
no fair game for me...
every time I lose the control
the rest have made me miss,
whenever my happiness needs to be shared
just because joy isn't the reason I want to weep.

So all this coming and going
can only lead us to 'good-bye',
it's true, indeed...
like a lifetime wasted over a flame that never was
burned long enough for its lovers to conceive.

What we leave behind is simply 'hello',
I regret to believe...
because my love is a blessing I plan to keep,
each time your happiness depends upon mine,
like the flesh becomes an accordian of muscles
our spirits choose to dance with...
as passion's music awakens both of us
with the energy of excitement's visible breeze.

For why I wish for happiness
is not my business but yours,
you see...
like your spirit creates Docetic attraction for me.
Because what creates physical ecstasy,
destroys mental agony,
or so it seems...
like eating lessens hunger's burning swell
and sleeping melts anger's winter freeze.

Still, as I spin around you perpetually,
you always manage to bring me to my knees...
and teach me how to romance
the second chances you trouble to make me see.
For as I begin to fear your voice,
until I end up with the hope of saying your name,
I feel the muse of poetry come back into me...
like roses bloom in emotional blood
whenever one thinks of beauty on Valentine's Day.

As I'm reminded of how our time together
could soon wind up being
nothing but faded memories,
I rush to make my poems pull you forever closer...
though the competition would have me desperate
to push you further away...
simply because our magic 'lives and dies' by the mystery
our actions meant to, yet our words refused to say.

Chauvinistic Personality Disorder

You see, the day has come for us
to pass greed on the road to lust.
Everybody has the power to belong to
whatever they decide they want to be.

You see, I was born with chauvinistic
personality disorder. My doctors prepare for me.

Then, when identity became a personal issue,
darkness and oblivion turned to paper and ink—
hours, into a bed of drowning think.

Through dead traffic lights, I was saved from the mad talk of Mom—
my sister singing *'Tom's Diner'* for procrastinated showers to bark.

Then came the alphabetization of sacred brick poetry,
the brink spark of vines wrapped around my firework heart—
unworthy wrongs never made heavy enough to sink.

Still on a 1999 porch, I put down the very first rights—
made 'no' weaker than 'yes', art more universal than life.

Though I took a while to sow what others allowed to grow,
I saw the extras of front pages on morning door steps,
went to window places, traced conversation's glass with apocalypse.

Until, angry beyond fatherly depression, I got better.
Investing nothing, you compromised all by spending your sanity
on me.

Glossing Over the Goddess Eyes of Grief

There is no existence in humanity's fallen Eden,
only the musk pulp that vortexes lust up from volcanoes
deep within the Devil's inhuman, remotely-childish heart.
There within man lies unfinished progress.

I have touched the frayed edges between Heaven and Hell,
pierced completely through its seamstress depths.
I have seen how a Goddess' eyes gloss over the surface of a man,
seen how she takes his hand deep inside hers as he double-takes

her fallen grace, stares into her well of grief, her dried well of affairs.
One midnight, one window quickly lifts along a sore man's crossroad
street.
A blinding kitchen light heals his swollen numb feet as they step
over tiles,
heal his cold bare feet as his job opens his refrigerator to hunger and
thirst.

Both call him there to sit and wait at its gate, fill his Omega gut with
culture.
He waits for the sun to return, waits to wake lost lovers back to their
seats.
He makes his table with toast, milk, and the fruits of Goddess grief
gloss.
Leave behind the crumbs of your nonexistence your needs will only
satisfy

the jealousy that refills intolerance's inhuman tank.
Drive off the early morning lacks with their taunt invisible reins
the ones that join howling dogs to hissing cats,
as their avocado skin goosebumps with the pulp of their polluted
skies,

peels back like your unrequited loves are unborn within your unlived past,
as clouds ripen with light, spoiling from red to brown;
as others vulture to learn the future's all-too-familiar task
the one that eventually rains down upon us with the sounds of bird song.

Moments of bliss and tactless hurts the old man's mind is a double-edged sword.
America's ancestors call us back, to take our Roanoke Island broken toy hearts,
dig past the moss of the Devil's dirt-cratered mound, find a reason worth living for.
Before dawn we will find out the truth, what really happened between me and you.

Unexciting the Iguana Female Trinity

He searches for her leaving a foreign plaza as the movie crowd slowly exits.

She has yet to read the play's poem, has yet to break her married ticket stub.

Her friend has opened her eyes to a life she is about to see as a compromise.

Yet under control is her touch and quick summary of *The Night of the Iguana.*

He grunts to himself as she comes up, smelling of third-party incense smoke.

A child greets them in a running Volkswagen *Beetle.* Their words sound old

as they argue the purposes of keeping one waiting, of keeping new jealousy.

Christ fills her mind with William's exciting play while reciting *Female Trinity.*

A curious woman looks at them from the lowest step, covers her perfect hair.

Iguana scales close his eyes as the man in the car notices what is happening.

From his island he departs, arrives to Berwyn Heights, to his apartment brick.

She thinks of Mary and Martha as she draws out for him the priest's dilemma,

draws out how flesh fought in vain, took *'the long swim to China'* to fight drink.

He lights up for a moment as her *Vaseline* purse-breaks her ticket stub bread.

He feels his bucket heart buckshot desire as he watches cold eyes fill with fire.

The child replaces fears with burning hope as he observes this in his backseat,

like the poor observe how staple needs slowly burn a budget, burn rich plastic
without the rest of finger couch TV or two *Three King's Day* fried eggs on rice.

Never Sleeps

Something in the way she calls me when I'm holding out for Omega glories,
the holy uploads that rise and fall like prepared lines for near-miss meals—
the microwave serving for pocketknife graces said over hotel-covered glass.

Never leaves keys and forever sleeps, like love and war ends without beginning.
We are the exhausted air of fear's fluid lives. Hope is a passing elimination.
Give yourself a piece of cake and the world may decide to eat you up instead.

She tells me by my gradual internal combustion that I am failing to avoid feelings.
Over my overpriced steak, she gets drunk, pays no dues for half-assed excuses.
She digs a tomb for her other blood-faced men— afraid to be late, yet womb-loose.

God leaves us alone long enough to discover *YouTube*'s unprotected, TV-posting.
Its message is our untaken journey, the one that wakes, like my dream of a friend
who came to my father's house. "I have an early doctor's appointment," he insists.
As his sleeping territory becomes snores, I relish our private cheer turned to shock.

There are many near-accidents. They enter shared, careless rooms, make you feel

like your mind is getting full with an ocean soup as you tell someone close, far away,
that you need to walk outside, show the rushing traffic that life, like art, never sleeps.

Yet in the beeping horns of opened window, dusk traffic, they tell you to *uck yourself.
You will gently reply the same to them someday. Only just pity them. Envy will rewind—
will let us see when they were of any help; will decide who lights their memory cigarette.

Chance Plane-Burns Provident Winter

(For my grandmother Inés Acevedo)

There beyond the carried loads of sacrificed resistance are the winters
of frictionless static.
A man returns to mother thinking of what the rooster starts, listening
to scratching-dog glass.
Her tears gather family as he speaks, hat in lap— smiles of life not
too brief, of suit-cased loss.

Some say the blues plane-burn tire fears like suitcase winter.
And I have seen them lie, pretend to offer the hopes the spring will
never get.

But there is something in the father's love that I have learned while
in its cold,
like the happiness of a hungry child depends upon the dependence
of the father
and the happiness of the mother upon the sanctity of an angry son.

Drones are dropping newspapers from cargo hooks onto the driveways
of undeparted cars.
Emanations of faith are but law and act to the first and the last, like
girls fisting candy cash.

Can you see past the sidewalk dusk, past the phone booth where she
returns to me?
I cannot answer her future's present call. The dime she inserts has
rusted way too thin.
Her hyper index finger cancels unatoned grief. A straight and narrow
year has passed.

Her renewed doubt is burning faith's tires in *New Balance* sneakers beside a roommate
as we cross her heated path, reminds me that chancing providence never gives pause.

You Are So Beautiful

You are so beautiful to me.
You are so beautiful to believe.
You are so beautiful to set free
Can't you see?

You are the forgotten sorrow
when morning becomes a mystery.
You are so beautiful to me.
I begged, stole, and borrowed
for the degree.
I kegged beer for the college
when they threw up on me.
You are the key-less starter,
the flash of memory.

You are so beautiful.
You danger me so beautiful,
I can't see
if the rose is dying,
if the close is just beginning.
Still, you are so beautiful to me.

Godzilla Globals Human Radiation

I had changed. Work and pity parties had moved
my soul to be saved by the life I never knew.
It was just a fluke, a misfired chance I mistook
that sent me into the future with a past to be glued.

Tonight the end justifies the means
when memory reverses mirror inverses as a child's tears
that scale cheeks to appear late enough to be redeemed,
as I fill a hole made whole like love, its crooked, tectonic plate ice.

She B-Line's wait with double-date, tailgate grief—
debunks the lost with unsaved costs.
Mourning is never late when dreams won't overtake,
like arms muscling for a pillow to wake collect-called sleep.

I accept her needs roar to endure yet mine only horseshoe more.

I'm losing my waist to worries.
I'm laughing my ass off to hurry.
The weather feels more chill than a morning coffee killed,
until Godzilla goes global with human radiation tonight.

I'm raking up bitterness with overdone tasks—
sipping soup because I did this loop way too fast.
I'm coughing my meds as my bumped-up microwave goes dead.
I'm only missed when I finally make others not want to ask.

I'm extending family change. I'm paying for interest not to Fed.
Smile your Hell all you want yet I must buy myself a shorter belt,
because the money don't pool love when funny rules-out help,
for your Godzilla to go global with human radiation tonight.

Trials never beguile. The trouble lies in love's double-standard miles. Keeping to yourself, you may come to finish what you get, bet regrets will leave you like worms thrown to screaming nests as Godzilla tests the theory that conception is but God's test, radiation struggle's death.

I accept her needs roar to endure yet mine only horseshoe more.

From a cold heart and pastel style comes secret news in what I say. She is many yet I see few. I hate the easy that smiles the hard play. Yet Bowie's road drives up class as I use *The Force* line under line, won over by fine girls with finger snaps, burn their bittersweet denial.

Turning to Ravel at a Roadblock

I'm listening for the tune
that races beyond a roadblock somewhere in Forest Glen, Maryland.
A sudden storm hits my windshield until the cars ahead of me stop.

A police officer does not wave at a single soul, his covered head
down.
One by one, we advance, as each car's driver decides to circle back.

I am slowly thinking of a familiar song I could never outlast.
Boléro is playing on a local Classical music station I was about to
pass,
as the road crossing Jericho's dark wreckage seems to join the
undergrowth.

A mother passes my car with an umbrella as the young victim's father
crouches over his son's stretched-out ashes and dust in the advancing
rain.

Inside my car, Ravel begins to move my wipers like a Scottish
marching drum.
His father fingers his son's remains on the pavement as a familiar
girl arrives.
I hear the crush of glass as I leave our brief past, leave my engine
running hot.

She must not be happy because, to her, doubt clues her into my hidden
signs.
She must be hurting because my ride seems to bridal an invisible
weight inside.

Somehow I can see the fear on her pale, wet face as the officer asks her name.
Somehow I can still smell the undying seed beneath the victim's khaki raincoat,
as I build a groom out of heaven for his sockless sneakers and annihilated face.

I can only hear my car's *Boléro* as the officer asks me if I knew the dead man.
"I only came over to see," I say, both of us a bit ashamed of the girl's smile.

Still, the officer adds not her absent strife in the young man's unresolved report.
Judge Ravel, if you must. Evidence pits wit against grit as mind and soul slowly fit
the crime as the other is judged for the thrill that baits for the kill of *Boléro*'s brass.

She requests that the officer move onto the task of dispersing the curious crowd.
Who does the competition turn to after seeing his flame burn his heartaches alive?

I'm listening for the tune
that races beyond a roadblock somewhere in Forest Glen, Maryland.
Where tarts peddle irreplaceable hearts and Sodom and Gomorrah settle to survive.

LA Don't Mess with my Old Man

I've seen my barber's child claw his paper plate with his fingertips,
claw for *Honey Nut Cheerios* as his Old Man clips off the LA channel.
"Now that's something else," he says. He flicks O's past straight hair.

The compact refrigerators sold well the two days after the hurricane.
The Korean did a Klingon salute, fist over chest, as my mother became me.
His wife tried to bring him over fuel loss clouds that kamikaze radioed plans,
cried in the way my eyes grew frightened as they smiled for something free.

I eat Farmer's Cheese from the Middle Eastern grocery shelf. It tastes rich.
Takes me back again to the visions of Zen recovered from my Carolina year,
the year my professor left a gift around underlined Christian white out type.
"Yes... sometimes that's all we can do" was her solution to meaninglessness.

Freedom is as arrogant as the vintage extension cord tangles relayed realities.
It's like the homeless trying to survive without one attached to premature beds.
The compact units never keep a place on the shelf. I still smile at sudden loss.
Send your son to meet in LA, Mister President. Don't mess with my Old Man.
The *Cheerio* chalk still O's the foreign plate. Rope whips its yoke vinyl cement.

Support Noon's Mana Mourning

When I wake to the light of day,
I learn— not before, yet now can see
how love becomes survival's sole support.

And like the bones I export
to the world of commercial greed,
love imports energy like noon mana's mourning.

I fall asleep as the world breaks down with heat.
That's when she calls me by text.
Every family cries with joy as she reports my progress.

So if she is to see me when I'm mad with jealous envy
as corporations shock Cheverly workers like electric psychology,
I only ask for the anomaly that perpetuates needs' proximities.

There is a dawn for every love that comes at the apex of life.
It is the mana of resurrection fight, a feeling so unlike failure's
absence—
the booths of close-call, last requests to honor the vacuumed presence.

We're Watching Her Show (3 A.M. Clicks)

I can almost stand now.
Uselessness has gotten lost over useful needs.
"There's something wrong with you," she had said.

She's always wrong and imperfect,
the reason she saved me.

God creates destruction for man.
Man destroys Creation for woman.
Waited on the crashing.
Forget about it, 'window man'!
Only she knows my rougher side. Hey,
Baby. Say whatcha want today. Fin?
You're cool.
I keep myself safe here in the bath.
Square as a jerk for ya.
I hear the dog start the talk as I cough.
Ugh!

Feel it right now.
Can't stop.
Is it really so or don't you wanna stay
just for the night?
I said those three words
without a thought of no.
She said I was: "not ready to be my friend."
So, now I watch 'Kinky' as 'The Catman'
and she has grown on me,
like "Not really" or "I know."
It's in my nature to sow
not just to tell you so.
The window light has gone off.
Goodnight until next time.
Ugh!

Singing 'Night Moves' while sitting on a green rock somewhere on the blue edge, somewhere in North Flanders, Belgium. She said: "What do you mean?" We're watching her show now.

Something I could never do. And I will fall for memories, when the night is young and you're with me. So let's get high on used-to-be's and call me up in reality. I may fall in reality. But let me stall our memories. Let me Saul my used-to-be's, and call you up in memories. You get high on poetry. So let me fly on 'owe-it-to-me.' Let me write a line for free. We watch her show us everything. So let me show what gets to me. You show me how to believe. So give me up for memories. You go to work for just a week. So show us all you still believe. Don't be a dog. Please let me be and wash yourself of enemies. I did my part. I hold the key. I bid you adieu. Watch for a light to shine on me. See her future fade to black. Take in the view as you look back.

How hard the rain must have hit, along with my coffee cup fists, the moment he got word of this, like bathroom sails of starched collars Church abyss, curtain call *The Temple of The Rising Sun*.

You can't give what you never knew.
Can't take what others don't.

You play me with games that have hurt me,
left me.
You say you're in love...
but I need big money plays.
You here what I hear,
bleed what I seed,
sing that beat that plays,
skunk my air with your sugar purrs.
What is it that makes us sad
when we think of effort?

I cry everytime.
Everytime.

"There's something wrong with you," she had said.
She's always wrong and imperfect,
the reason she saved me.

Sometimes eye sockets get blind like smoke,
sometimes souls get lost to cigarette break cold.
Empty your pockets of life's ungotten joke--
the miles and miles of paper smiles
that pick up big customers without saying a word,
leave their circles,
their sanctified holes that implode celibacy,
stay open for business until you cannot cope,
deposit dust like spirit bones 3 A.M. Manteo ash
with long-delayed checks that finally come with love,
yet will never get cashed.

Soap your destruction with the hope my salt.

All this suffering
just because all want justice
over the one who pays the dues of one.
My so-called 'issues' with stem from 'woman'
not from 'man'.
Just because you don't want me
should not make me into an enemy,
be it sexual or otherwise.

Thank you Heavenly Father for this gift
you have disturbed with and revealed unto me.
It came from hurt and has healed.
It will return as seed back into the Universe.
For it comes from Thine wind and dirt.
Those who have eyes, see!
Those who have ears, hear!
Those who can believe, know!

What is it that makes us sad to think of new needs?

You can't give what you never knew.
Can't take what others don't.

I cry everytime.
Everytime, Baby.

I guess the way you know me
is whenever you laugh at someone you really need.

The problem is that my tears are for me.

This pre-dawn morning I sit in a Fayetteville bathtub
until Hall & Oates' 'She's Gone' fades with the battery...
until I'm self-maiding slow, tricking myself, stand up.

Nietzsche's Speech at Gettysburg
(for Ben and Dorothy)

There is something sweet in the unsaid,
something that grief cannot make into speech.
There is a feeling I have felt in the roaming mountains,
in a soldier's faultless uneaten sandwich bread,
the daughter opening it to see what he has addressed,
the depleted layers of raked ozone, the Socialism of Nietzsche.

I sit up in my Hilton bed. It is midnight here at Gettysburg,
"I Keep Forgettin' (Every Time You're Near)" MP3's the radio.
My head drops from mysteries as the TV counts election votes,
the *'Four Score'* poetry by Lincoln still marching in my head.
I am marching to the Boston Pops, to sacrifice, marching with Dad.
There is something I have yet to say, something of Mary Magdalene.

A house becomes undivided after something like this is claimed,
after one hears Sanders denounce the Party as CNN unrolls sleeves.
I am resting with Nietzsche as working legs muscle processed sheets,
process grand finales, late returns, process fully-baked quarterly cheese.
Morning bills cookie doe leads across a fallen America as we sleep.
As for justice, there is nothing led or *"fallen too short"*, nothing to speak.

Copernicus Sleeps So Far

I would ascend her and she would scream:
"To not be a lover is not to be!"
Now I wake like Copernicus, so far from dreams,
subways juice deleted tracks as bags leave hosed streets.
Jay-Z untrumps Trump and the spiritual center of Galileo.
Jimmy Kimmel trumpets American flesh and blood affairs.
I know my feelings are hurt.
I know that my heart won't restart.
I know how emotions never part.
But I give just like a man.
I take just like a woman.
I live just like a child.
But I make love only to myself.
Because she's always a woman.
He's always her man.
We're always willing.
But the buck stops with her hand.
So I know her feelings are hurt.
I know her heart must start again.
I know the emotion that never can part.
I've been murdered just like a victim.
I've been robbed just like a Cop.
I've heard the alphabet of every survivor
every time I pick up from where you left off.
I keep all your lessons forever in my head.
I leave them to anyone who needs to be helped.
Steep are the steps where you will have to go.
Maybe I have forgotten
who has helped others to leave you alone.
But I know just like a fool.
I take just to break another's rule.
I suffer just like a woman.
I heal just like a man.

I kill just like a market.
I fall just like Adam without his will.
The job may be hairy.
The mob of my fans may always be small.
But you'll feel just like a woman.
You'll steal just like a Cop.
You'll breathe just like in a vacuum
when you Altar your world for the girl they never saw.
Now I wake like Copernicus, so far from dreams,
subways juice deleted tracks as bags leave hosed streets
as Kim Kardashian smiles for off-center cameras in America
and Guillermo hugs for tequila and Desert Storm autographs.

Soul Attraction

I could have died for you,
and yet...

Since pushing through the rains of pouring train's unrequited stop:
my traveling asteroids anchored; my oxidized thoughts sheathing by
lust:
I've sentimentalized pain. Thorned are dreams: some lived, some
lied, most lost.

I could have relied on you,
and yet...

Since love's frustration-earthquakes,
my soul has healed body and mind:
letting one give what the other takes; saving me by the truth God has
made rhyme.

I could have defied you,
and yet...

Since falling in and out of love,
I've fallen in and out of grace.
Found that debts are bought within and walked dress shoes along a
sea of moss.

I could have decided on you,
and yet...

Since Monet's paintings have been salvaged by Nag Hammadi
politicians,
I've seen the snow blight his poppies, overextend parasols, numb
cheeks with rage.

The Outer Banks lighthouse sage is she: spoken for by limbless trees
of solemn weight.
I could have done all of this,
and yet...

Since waltzing beside your gait,
I've lived in mirth, another man:
still redeeming this premature fate; still praising you from these
disciple hands.

Sir:

~~This letter I am writing in to I would~~
~~like you~~ I'll be a graduate student in Physics
starting next sept and I ~~will~~ would like to have information
regarding the dates classes will be starting.
I was also offered a graduate Assistanship & I would
like to know what my responsibilities will be and
~~then and to whom I will~~ when & to whom I will
have to report for work.

also
I would like to use this letter to ask you ~~about~~
~~a letter~~ about night school since my future wife will like
to attend classes ~~starting~~ this sept ~~also~~. She would
to
be a sophomore in the pre-medical course

~~hoping to hear soon from you~~ Thank you for your
attention. I hope to hear soon from you.

respectfully yours,

F.S.

263

John Patrick Acevedo is extremely grateful to his family, friends, teachers, and fans for allowing him the awesome opportunity to share his *ethos* poems, written between 2010 and 2018.

Of the 123 poems appearing in this book, most have appeared in previous *Synergy Press* (*synergy-press.org*) books published by John Patrick Acevedo between 2012 and 2018. In 2003, before being reworked and featured in his book *"Ice A.D. Apex Delivery"*, Acevedo's poem *Volcanic Gravity* was published by *Gitana Press,* and some of his poems have appeared on *google. com*. A 2014 mini-documentary entitled *Windows Into Poetry* on Acevedo's poetic beginnings was produced by Prince Kwasi Mensah for *youtube.com* and a poem *Lares Vines, Monarch Cries* pays homage to Puerto Rican grandfather Juan Acevedo (*Really Naps the Maitre D*).

In 2008, the *Howard Community College Times* published *Siren Song*, a poem about capitalism through Native American eyes. Acevedo's video-poem *Virginal Vixen Distinction* is featured on *youtube.com* and has recorded six of his poems on a *spoken word* cd to promote the now-defunct poetry critique group the Wineglass Court Poets. In 2013, his powerful 14-poem recorded reading called *The Mad City Coffee Reading* was also published.

In 2009, during the *Poets and Painters* exhibit in Columbia, MD by the *Artists' Gallery*, his poem *Skeleton Swing* was featured. It describes a father's tragic loss of a daughter and the mesmerizing scenes of Maui that keep them together. In 2011, his poem *Mushroom Cloud Metamorphosis* was also exhibited at the gallery. In this poem, Acevedo answers the possessive will of youth by the wisdom of the aged, as a family celebrates the birth of a great-grandchild. In 2013, Acevedo's poems *Deer of the Crossing Last Ones,* a biblical look at the responsibility we face to meet the needs of those barely given a chance at salvation, and *Salmon Memory*, a spiritual piece on the salmon's dying journey to the place of its birth, were exhibited at the gallery as well.

In 2016, Acevedo published his motion picture short *Holy Bible Sociology! A Journey into the Soul of John Patrick Acevedo* on *youtube.com*. It lays down the foundation to a 30-year metaphysical metamorphosis that began in 1982 with Marvin Gaye's *Sexual Healing*.

"If I ever thought 'give and take' dropped by my lonely father after a Seinfeld TV episode on an unwanted Friday phone call while renting a porch for a room in Forest Glen, Maryland in 1991 would be the 'Soul Attraction' by which all of my ascetic self-doubts could become the poetry of my gnostic salvation, I would have said: 'Really?'" Acevedo jokes.

John Patrick Acevedo is a graduate of Boston University and was a consistent top sales performer with Best Buy for 20 years. Acevedo writes poetry in his hometown of Columbia, MD. He promotes his books at local libraries and bookstores. His latest book entitled *We're Watching Her Show (For Bathroom Sails of the Starched Collar): The Ethos of John Patrick Acevedo, (Synergy/Xlibris Press, 2018)* will be reviewed by The New York Times for its Christmas issue. To order more books by John Patrick Acevedo, please visit us on *Synergy Press'* eStore/website at *market.synergy-press.org/synergy-press.org.*